The Goddess and the Bull

A Study in Minoan-Mycenaean Mythology

Helen Benigni and Barbara Carter

Edited with a foreword by
Miriam Robbins Dexter

UNIVERSITY PRESS OF AMERICA, INC.
Lanham • Boulder • New York • Toronto • Plymouth, UK

Copyright © 2007 by
University Press of America,® Inc.
4501 Forbes Boulevard
Suite 200
Lanham, Maryland 20706
UPA Acquisitions Department (301) 459-3366

Estover Road
Plymouth PL6 7PY
United Kingdom

Library of Congress Control Number: 2007933749
ISBN-13: 978-0-7618-3834-0 (paperback : alk. paper)
ISBN-10: 0-7618-3834-1 (paperback : alk. paper)

In honor of

Eadhmonn Ua Cuinn
(1938–   )

Contents

Foreword   vii

Preface   xi

Acknowledgments   xvii

1   The Doors of Precession   1

2   The Astronomer Priestesses of the Bronze Age   17

3   The Goddess and the Bull   33

4   Time-Keepers   51

Appendixes   73

Works Cited   87

Bibliography   91

Index   95

About the Authors   99

Foreword

This book is a continuation of the authors' former research in, *The Myth of the Year*, a fascinating look at animal forms of the prehistoric and early historic goddesses. Whereas the focus on the first volume was on bird and snake figures, the focus here is on the myth and iconography of the goddess and the bull, complemented as before by intriguing astronomical and cosmological evidence. Seasonal myth and ritual is here connected to the constellations which appear at different times of the year, once again uniting the terrestrial with the cosmic, and thus deepening the sacred meanings of the seasons.

The bull, reflected in the sky as the constellation of Taurus, appears in the winter sky. Its horns stretch toward the west, toward the ram, Aries. The bull is accompanied in early historic myth and iconography by a consort, the Great-Goddess as cow. It was very likely important in the early prehistory of homo sapiens sapiens as well: in the Indo-European languages, *taurus* can mean bull, ox, or bison, and one may think of the cave art at Upper Palaeolithic sites such as Lascaux, where bison are depicted.

Both myth and iconography attempt to explain and depict what ancient peoples saw in the sky. One of the most salient depictions of taurine iconography is the bucranium, the bull's or cow's horn.

The use of bucrania as ritual art becomes prominent in the early Neolithic, and it is an important marker of ancient religion, having a broad geographic base. An early, pre-Neolithic site in Anatolia, Göbekli Tepe, in southeastern Turkey, dating to ca. 9000 BCE, contained pillars on which were carved reliefs of several animals, including a bucranium. Its excavator, Claus Schmidt, believes that it was a purely ritual site,[1] since no evidence of habitation, such as ovens or fireplaces, has been found. Thus the bucranium here must be connected with the spiritual beliefs of these peoples.

At the Neolithic site of Çatalhöyük, in the Konya Plain of Turkey—another site in ancient Anatolia—bucrania are modeled on the walls of many structures. According to one of the excavators, Naomi Hamilton, some of the animal horns are known to come from females.[2] Thus both female and male cattle were important to the peoples of Çatalhöyük. At Hacılar, near Lake Burdur, a site west of Çatalhöyük, dating from 7000–5000 BCE, the bucranium is found as well.[3]

One ancient Anatolian culture became important to the spread of the religion of the goddess Kubele/Cybele: Pessinus, in Western Turkey, ancient Phrygia. Wandering through its ancient cemetery, I came upon bucrania decorating many of the gravestones.

Perhaps the most famous culture which ritually depicts bucrania is that of the Minoans on Crete. Bucrania, sometimes called the "horns of consecration," are found on the walls of the Minoan temple complex dating to the second millennium BCE at Heraklion; structures in the Minoan colony of Akrotiri on the island of Santorini bear the same bucrania.

The ritual use of bucrania is not limited to the Circum-Mediterranean and the Near East. It is also found far to the East, in the Tarim Basin, west of China. In the cemetery called Ordek's Necropolis, also called SRC5, bucrania decorate several burials.[4]

The importance of cow as well as bull is seen in the religious pantheons of both Near Eastern and Indo-European cultures. So in Ugaritic myth the goddess Anat may have metamorphosed into a cow and borne to her 'brother', the fertilizing rain-god, 'bull-Ba'al', an ox.[5] The Egyptian goddess Hathor was depicted as a cow, and cow's horns comprise a part of her headdress. The Greek Hera was "cow-eyed." In Greek myth the thunder-god Zeus, consort of Hera, sometimes took the form of a bull; in one myth Zeus, having metamorphosed into a white bull, abducted the Phoenician Europa, carrying her off to Crete. Further, Hera is closely tied to the phases of the moon: she passes through three life phases—"child, mature woman, old woman" (*pais, teleia, chera*)—new, waxing, and waning moon.

The goddess as cow is found in more than one epiphany in Ireland as well. In the Irish epic, the *Táin Bó Cuailnge*, the ferocious goddess of regeneration, the Morrígan, appears to the hero Cú Chulainn in many forms, including that of a white cow. Another Irish text, the *Lebor Gabála Érenn,* names the goddess Boann, one of the mystical Tuatha Dé Danann—the "people of the goddess Danu;" for Boann, whose name contains the Irish word for 'cow', the river Boyne is named.

Before the Roman era, most calendars followed the nineteen-year cycles of moon and sun, in harmony with much astronomical phenomena. Since the Roman era, the focus of the calendar has been on the sun. This focus on light and day, without a corresponding focus upon darkness and night, is a symptom of the disconnectedness of our society from full integration with our planet and cosmos. As societies have become more urbanized, we have lost much of our understanding of and connection to the earth, the calendar, and the seasons. A return to a fuller understanding of the galaxies, the interconnectedness of the earth with the celestial phenomena which surround it, and the spiritual systems which have sought to explain it, can bring us into a greater wholeness with the realities of our world and a greater harmony with all the phenomena which surround us.

Miriam Robbins Dexter

NOTES

1. Klaus Schmidt, 2000, "Göbekli Tepe, southeastern Turkey. A Preliminary Report on the 1995–1999 Excavation." *Paléorient* 26,1: 46.

2. Naomi Hamilton, 1996, "Figurines, Clay Balls, Small Finds and Burials." In *On the Surface: Çatalhöyük 1993–95*. Ian Hodder, ed. Cambridge: McDonald Institute for Archaeological Research and British Institute of Archaeology at Ankara: 226

3. James Mellaart, 1965, *Earliest Civilizations of the Near East*. New York: McGraw-Hill: 120; James Mellaart, 1970, Excavations at Hacilar, passim. Edinburgh: Edinburgh University Press.

4. See Victor Mair, "The Rediscovery and Complete Excavation of Ordek's Necropolis." 2006. *Journal of Indo-European Studies* 34 (3–4): 283; 285. A large quantity of bovine as well as ovicaprid horns, found in the area, may have been left over from sacrifices (284).

5. *Keilschriftliche Texte aus Ugarit* (KTU) 1.10.ii–iii (+UT 76). See Miriam Dexter, *Whence theGoddesses: A Source Book*. New York: Pergamon, 1990: 29; 201.

Preface

The study of cross-cultural symbols gained a new impetus with the coining of the term "archetype" by Carl Gustav Jung. Although early psychologists such as Jung, attributed the formation of archetypes to a collective mind that gathered symbols through time, transferring them from one culture to another, a less romantic ideology of the formation of archetypes came to light. Without ignoring the genius of Jung, the mystery of the conception of the archetype might not be entirely lost. However, the actual historical process comes to the surface in modern studies with archeological evidence in the forefront. By keeping the original conception of the archetype as something deep, mysterious, and evidently embedded in our psyche and combining that idea with scientific data, perhaps the study of archetypes will strengthen our understanding of this cultural phenomenon. With this in mind, the discovery of new archetypes is entirely possible as an interdisciplinary effort.

Recently, the study of archeology has been combined with the study of astronomy to form a new discipline: archeoastronomy. Archeoastronomy or the study of ancient ruins and their alignment to the night sky has opened the possibility of yet another understanding of the archetype. With the addition of archeoastronomy to the study of the archetype as archeology, not withstanding and never losing the mystique of the human imagination, the study of archetypes is only enhanced by the symbols of time, those that reflect the patterns in the night sky as well as those that reflect the patterns of the earth. The archeological icons of a culture, the myths of a culture, and the symbols of a culture all contribute to the study of the archetype and create a well-balanced idea of what might have been represented by a culture. Many leaps of the imagination are needed to re-create such images and symbols and compare them throughout the history of one culture or through two cultures. The ultimate problem and perhaps the hesitancy on the part of much research has been the reluctance to combine psychology and the humanities with the hard sciences because one requires speculative imagination, forethought and presumption while the other determines an objective account of the facts to form conclusions, respectively. The difficult practice of the mind, to combine scientific efforts and speculative thought, must be overcome if research is to move forward, or ironically, move backward, to examine ancient cultures because this is most likely the way in which the ancients viewed their reality, as a coherent whole without disparate parts.

In this study of a newly discovered archetype, merging mythology with archeoastronomy has been the major effort. Underlying the myths is the scientific data, the charting of the moon, the sun, the stars, and their patterns in the sky. Numbers, data, and patterns emerge accompanied by an image, an archetype. Throughout mythology, the same constant appears. Recognizing it through the pattern of the moon, the sun, and the stars in one year gave way to the study of the cycles of the heavenly bodies in their cycles beyond the year. The doors of precession have been opened and the study of archetypes renewed. Even the study of the archetypes of the celestial within the year has been an organization of already established symbols to form a coherent whole following the patterns of the stars, the moon and the sun through the seasons of one year. The cycles that open the doors of precession or reveal the precessional cycles beyond the year begin with a newly discovered yet historically ancient archetype: The Goddess and the Bull. In this study, not only has a new icon come to light, possible by the merging of the disciplines of psychology, comparative mythology, archeology and astronomy, but boundaries between disciplines have been broken in order to conceptualize and ultimately to attempt to understand our ancestors and the way they thought. For the future of research and human understanding, this opens the doors of the imagination as well as the doors in our mind to the cycles of precession.

Seemingly, the human mind has forgotten that the patterns of the year as well as those patterns that go beyond the year are relevant and worth forming into archetypes that aid our understanding of our relationship with the natural world. The archetypes of precession, numerous as they are and yet buried as they are in myth and culture, have revealed themselves with the most obvious cycle first: the cycle of the ever changing moon. It is here where humans in Paleolithic times first began to count and conceptualize how the changing moon would affect their lives. Amazingly, our ancestors this far back in time, at the beginning of our realization of the connection between the starry dynamo and ourselves, came to the awareness that beyond the twelve cycles of the lunar year are the nutation cycle of the moon, where the moon rises in a different place on the horizon for 18.6 years and then returns forming a cycle of life. Added to this concept was the discovery that at nineteen years the sun meets the moon in its journey. Moreover, three of these lunar and solar cycles made up the lifetime of prehistoric humans. The archetype of these cycles of renewal upon which human life is based became paramount and was assigned to the creator of life, The Goddess, and her consort, the bison, or later, the domesticated bison, the Bull.

In the Paleolithic Era, The Goddess holds a bison horn which marks the cycles of precession. In the Neolithic Era, The Goddess has many symbols of regeneration to accompany her Bucrania or bull's horns, and The Horns of the Bull become consecrated in the Neolithic temples of The Goddess. The emerging archetype of the Bronze Age Goddess and the Bull, which is measured on the Bucrania or The Horns of Consecration of the Mediterranean peoples, is paramount to the Minoan-Mycenaean culture. In the Knossos temple-complex of the Mother Goddess of Crete as well as in the temple-complexes of the Minoan-Mycenaean culture on the mainland in Greece, The Goddess and the Bull reach heights of importance and dominate the iconography. In the Bronze Age at this time in Europe and the British Isles, The Goddess and the Bull are prevalent in the iconography but relatively less important than the celestial events that accompany the archetype, which are measured on the stones of time. The amazing feats of the megalithic stone constructions of Bronze Age Europe and the British Isles, such as the building of the Aubrey Circle at Stonehenge, emphasize the advancement of the science and technology as well as the worship of The Goddess and the Bull in this culture.

Because the archetype of The Goddess and the Bull was of such great importance to the Bronze Age peoples of the Mediterranean, they chose to use it as a central image in their religious practices. Again, the modern interpretation of the disciplines as separate and the emerging ideology of the patriarchy where female deities were of secondary importance prevented a complete study of this archetype. Sir Arthur Evans and Martin P. Nilsson in the first half of the Twentieth Century did extensive excavations of the Minoan-Mycenaean culture, faithfully recording the details of their studies as archeologists yet ignoring the celestial alignments and the importance of the feminine in the culture. Unfortunately, the seven volume set of Evans' work is now out of print and not accessible to the modern reader. By examining Evans's study as well as the works of Nilsson and by visiting the sites, the iconology of The Goddess and the Bull became evident to me and could be put in perspective. Evans records the archeological data of The Mother Goddess but ignores the role of the astronomer priestesses in the religion. Furthermore, his sees the temple-complex as a king's palace, an Iron Age concept that evolved much later with the emergence of the patriarchy. The absence of a divine king or priest is evident in the archeological data; however, in his era, Evans viewed data through the eyes of the firmly established patriarchy of the Mid-Twentieth Century. Fortunately, Evans did establish that The Goddess was a Mother Goddess.

The Mother Goddess of the Minoan-Mycenaean culture emerges from the dust of ages and astounds our imagination, which has been throttled by the possibility that anything but a monotheistic father-god might exist. Without a father god or a king, the Mother Goddess, her young male consort, her astronomer priestesses, and the energies of the earth and heavens represented in the sacrifice of the Bull come to light as genuinely central to the culture. Moreover, in the nineteen year cycle of the moon and the sun, The Goddess is represented as a mother with the obvious capabilities to regenerate and continue the cycles of the earth as they correspond with the cycles of the heavens. Seen as a source for renewal, she is rarely personified on a grand scale and subsequently remains a representative force of Nature. Only one massive statue has been un-earthed from the Minoan-Mycenaean temple-complexes that demonstrate her presence on a large scale as compared to the many large statues of goddesses in later civilizations, such as the Greek and the Celtic cultures. In Minoan-Mycenaean culture, her iconology takes the form of many small goddess figurines among countless artifacts with her image as a seated, maternal figure much like later representations of Hera, in the Greek Iron Age, and the Matrona, in the Celtic Iron Age. Furthermore in Minoan-Mycenaean culture, her surname remains "po-ti-ni-ja", and her forenames are listed according to her attributes as bride or snake goddess in the Mycenaean Linear B tablets; as further evidence of the goddess' presence, it is notable that the tablets at Knossos only mention priestesses and not priests. Again, her common surname as a pre-Hellenic goddess emphasizes her tendency to be seen as seemingly almost monotheistic rather than polytheistic and clearly personified.

As a pre-Hera figure, The Goddess embodies the form of an omnipresent force of Nature, even in her bride aspect. Although her later associations with deities in the Iron Age in Greece, such as her name as Eileithyia, Britomartis, and Ariadne, are presented in maiden form, this does not take away from the fact that the bride aspect of the Mother Goddess of the Bronze Age was in fact a maiden about to join forces through the sacred marriage with the male in the form of a bull to regenerate the cycle of the moon and the sun. Birthing of the cycle becomes of utmost importance and the maiden must give herself through marriage to the cycles of birth and re-birth in the heavens as well as on earth. This aspect as well as her aspect depicting the Chthonic forces represented in the snake and her Earth forces represented in the form of the lion or the sphinx make her image not only pervading, but unique. The idea of a female sphinx is as different to the cultures with emerging patriarchies as is the idea of an omnipotent feminine deity. The idea of a pre-Hellenic, pre-Hera, goddess culture must be considered as a possibility in the same way that the possibility of any deity, symbol or archetype connected to the heavens existed in order that a holistic approach to the study of the ancients arise in our culture. The Queen of Heaven and Earth on her throne surrounded by her mythical beasts is a concept that opens the doors of perception and the doors of precession.

With the emergence of the patriarchy, kingship and organized warfare in the Iron Age, the archetype of The Goddess and the Bull evolves as a symbol of male regeneration in association with kingship, with the forces of the goddess still present. The sacrifice of the bull in Classical Greece is the sacrifice of Dionysus as the Bull accompanied by his earth mother, Semele, the Maenads, his priestesses, and his wife, Ariadne. Likewise, the sacrifice of the bull in Iron Age Europe is best portrayed by Queen Maeve of the *Táin Bó Cuailnge*, or the Battle of the Bulls. Here, the goddess-like Queen is still the intoxicating female who regenerates the nineteen year cycle of the moon and the sun in her quest for the fertile forces of the bull and her connection to the land as mother of the earth. In a final representation of the nineteen year cycle of precession, the Celts and the Druids, their priestesses and priests, sacrificed the bull to the goddess in their calendar celebrations but depicted the cycle itself as a process of rejuvenation inspired by the goddess and practiced by the Druid Bards. Amergin and Taliesin, the great mythical Celtic Bards, move the cycle into poetry and see it as the metempsychosis or series of lifetimes of the spiritually enlightened. In the abstract, it is still the renewal of life and the celebration of life, death and re-birth.

Perhaps, the study of the archetype of The Goddess and the Bull, after prefacing the necessary changes in research and thought, is most attuned to through an understanding of the intelligence of our ancestors. It is here that the completion of the archetype and the possibility of the study of other similar archetypes will take place. Archetypes of the planets and the constellations within the context of mythology, archeology and astronomy are only possible with the acceptance that our ancestors possessed a complete and accurate knowledge of the precessional cycles, a knowledge evident to us only as a knowledge of facts. Only by relating the facts of astronomy to religion, philosophy and comparative cultural studies, will the full potential of our imaginations be utilized and our relationship with the forces of the earth be appreciated and kept in balance, a respect sorely needed in today's economy of diminishing natural resources. This may be realized through two Iron Age devices that record the cycles of precession: The Antikythera Device of the Mediterranean and the Coligny Calendar of Europe. The discovery of the Antikythera Device in the Mediterranean reveals the knowledge of the cycles of precession including the nineteen year cycle of the moon and the sun. Likewise, the Coligny Calendar, discovered in France, is a device that measures the cycles of time into eternity. A translation of the Coligny calendar has revealed the knowledge of the ancients in the myths of the year. The iconology of the year in the text *The Myth of the Year: Returning to the Origin of the Druid Calendar* (Benigni, Carter, and Ua Cuinn. Lanham: University Press of America, 2003) reveals the myths of the year through comparative mythology and archeoastronomy. In this text, *The Goddess and the Bull: A Study in Minoan-Mycenaean Mythology,* the first precessional cycle, the nineteen year cycle of The Goddess and the Bull, begins by opening the doors of precession. By carefully measuring the moon in The Horns of Taurus, the constellation of the bull in the night sky at the Winter Solstice in its precessional cycle, we have opened the doors of future study to the patterns of the moon, the sun, the stars and the planets and our relation to them.

Helen Benigni
Elkins, West Virginia, 2007

Acknowledgments

I am thankful for the love and support of my dear friend and companion, Eadhmonn Ua Cuinn who has been a great part of the mind that conceived the myth and meaning behind the nineteen year cycle of the moon. I am indebted to Sir Arthur Evans for his undying love of ancient culture and his attention to detail.

As always, Miriam Robbins Dexter has offered her love, support, and immense talents to my efforts. Special thanks to Bob McCutcheon for his editing expertise and patience teaching grammar to an old grammarian.

Gratitude also goes to Kyli Catlett, my research assistant, and to all the people, especially my students, my two daughters, Amanda and Emily, and to my husband, Tyler Lutz, and my friends who support me.

Thanks also to Mark Butervaugh, the artist of both the cover and the interpretations of Minoan-Mycenaean art before each chapter. His talent and expertise is much appreciated.

Finally, I would like to acknowledge the efforts of the major participant in an on-going project to enlighten others as to the cycles of the ancients in the night sky. Barbara Carter is the genius behind the astronomy. Her calculations and insights, and her eternal counting and re-counting of the moon, the sun and the stars have been of the greatest help to this study. Without her efforts and kind guidance, I would not have been able to write this book or the first book in the journey.

Helen Benigni 1/13/07

Chapter One

The Doors of Precession

The doors of precession were opened by our ancestors eons ago when our deepest sense of the infinite was reaffirmed through scientific observation and the belief in something much larger and more powerful than ourselves. The moon afforded our first glimpses of eternity through careful observation of its changing face. Not only did it act as a guide through the seasons of the year, but miraculously, the moon showed change over longer periods of time. The doors to the precessional cycles of the moon and the stars were accessible and the worship began. Both woman and man became a vital part of the process, and the moon became a symbol of life, death and regeneration. As progenitor of growth, the moon opened the doors to the mystery of time, and the evidence of the moon's power over the ebb and flow of the tides, over the lives of plants and animals, and over the human cycles took definite mythological form.

In the Paleolithic Era, the first moon goddess appears holding the horn of a bison or auroch. Known to archeologists as the Venus of Laussel, Dordogne, France this figure portrays the moon's growth cycle from the newly crescent moon to the full moon in the thirteen vertical strokes on her elevated bison horn. Here, we have firmly established two concepts that will remain constant from the Paleolithic Era of approximately 23,000 BC to the Bronze Age. The first concept is that the moon is a power of regeneration of life from death, a parallel made from observing the growth of the moon from the new moon to the full moon with the growth of plants and with the growth of humans; the goddess's left hand draws the viewer's attention to her womb indicating the parallel to the growth of life itself. The second concept is the idea that the moon and the bison are one in the same power. Therefore, the process of re-generation of life from death or the creation of life itself must involve both a feminine and a masculine force as the bison is an adept representation of the fecund power of the masculine.

The sacredness of the number thirteen also identifies lunar cycles beyond their monthly course. Every two and one half years, a thirteenth moon occurs in order for lunar time to be in sync with the journey of the sun throughout the year. In the context of Paleolithic art, early humans were most interested in depicting what Joseph Campbell describes as a "timeless idol of the nature religions" where humanity records the unusual or the aberrant as forms of nature worthy of deification (*Transformations of Myth* I). The thirteenth moon held by the goddess is just such a "timeless idol" because it allows us to believe in the unusual or magnificent departure of nature from the aesthetic field of concrete abstraction to the dramatically different, a concept indigenous to Paleolithic art.

The shift from the timeless idol of nature in the Paleolithic art to the abstract and temporarily ordered process of Neolithic art is as remarkable as the shift from a cyclical to a linear understanding of time and history from ancient times to the present. We harken back to our first recognition of the counterparts between the celestial and the earthly in the figure of Laussel with an understanding of how much we have changed. As W.B. Yeats outlines in his book *A Vision*, the moon must remain the primary mask in the development of our lives (78–81). Our first moon goddess and bison's horn is therefore understandably part of a group of four of goddesses which might possibly represent each mask we must don or each of the four phases of the moon: first quarter, full, last quarter and new. Unfortunately, little detail on the figures in low relief is clearly discernible other than the fact that two of the four elevate an object and the fourth is a mirror image of herself (Leroi-Gourhan 303).

However, the one perceptible image of our goddess with the thirteen strokes on the bison's horn might be the most telling. In an astounding work of archeoastronomy, *Sun, Moon and Stonehenge*, Robin Heath remarks that the number thirteen is "a very lunar number." Heath reminds us that our own age has lost track of the larger cycles of the precession of the stars at the vernal equinox where each 2,000 years is measured by the rising constellation at the vernal equinox. The Taurean Age or the Age of the Bull, from approximately 4,000 to 2,000 BC, was an era ruled by Venus with the Moon exalted. The worship, that perhaps is even older than this recorded time with its roots reaching into the Paleolithic Era, was eventually dissipated by the Iron Age, or the Age of Aries, and then the modern age, or the Age of Pisces which "threw out the Goddess religions, and anything lunar automatically went out with the package" (Heath 33). The precessional cycles, divisible by thirteen to yield exact 2000 year periods, were ignored, and we were no longer interested in "the realities which inform us that there should be thirteen ages." Likewise, the fact that the moon moves just over thirteen degrees a day around the earth, and the fact that it makes just over thirteen orbits in one solar year, clearly visible to a causal observer, have also been ignored (Heath 34). With this in mind, our goddess' thirteen takes on deeper significance and leaves us to ponder exactly how much our ancestors were aware of the cycles of precession.

When the Paleolithic period of cave sanctuaries gives way to the emergence of the city civilizations of the Neolithic Era, the belief in the moon goddess and her bison remains a dominant motif with some adaptations. Here, notes Campbell, "a remarkable thing happens in certain places and certain times, namely the timeless idol of the nature religions yields to a temporally ordered process so that civilizations emerge that have histories, a youth, a maturity and an aging" (*Transformations of Myth* I). With this emphasis on time and its continuum, it is no wonder that the goddess and the bull, now a domesticated bison that needs protection and food, become a central image of the Neolithic culture at places such as Çatal Hüyük. New images of bucrania and other depiction of bulls are still associated with time, regeneration, birthing and, of course, the moon, when the bison or auroch now extinct in the nearby Taurus Mountains and on the Konya Plain are replaced by the image of the bull. The Goddess and the Bull have evolved, yet they retain much of their former symbolic value.

In a study of *The Goddess of Anatolia*, James Mellaart remarks that the bull is now represented by its head alone in many of the temples at Çatal Hüyük. He offers several sound reasons for this. First, Mellaart states, the bull's head emerges from the goddess in her birthing position as a frontal representation of the actual birth process and that the uterus with its fallopian tubes looks remarkably like a bull's head, hence the choice of the bull's heads at Çatal Hüyük. Mellaart refers to an earlier study of birth and death symbols in the Neolithic done by D.O. Cameron where she diagrams the female organs of reproduction clearly illustrating their similarity to the bull's head and horns where even the infundibulum or flower-like ends of the fallopian tubes appear as rosettes in Neolithic art complementing this "potent symbol of generation, never entirely replaced by the later patriarchal phallic symbol" (9). Miriam Robbins Dexter suggests that perhaps, the rosettes might also be symbolic of the morning and evening star adding yet another feminine reference to their overall meaning. Mellaart does comment on a reference to astronomy when he asserts that the bull's horns most likely represent the moon in its waxing and waning stages and are associated with the regeneration of the life forces such as women's menstrual cycles and water as a source of life (23). Likewise, Campbell states that the bull's heads at Çatal Hüyük are representations of the moon dying and being resurrected again through the "birth giving form" of the goddess where the mother receives us in death and the mother brings us into life (*Transformations of Myth* I). Through these analyses and possibilities, a myriad of images reflects the many meanings inherent in this feminine and potent maternal symbol.

Although the goddess is portrayed as the mother in her birthing form, she might also be considered as consort and lover to the bull. In Neolithic symbology, the goddess figures are transformers of the life force in a dual role as both mother and lover. This is best represented in a relief of the goddess discovered at Çatal Hüyük where the goddess is back-to-back with herself embracing a male on the left side and holding a child on the right. As the center of the agricultural and emotional life of the community, the goddess acts as the key symbol of the mythology. She is "the primary mythological figure personifying the energies of nature which transform past into future, semen into child, seed into produce, and so forth" (Campbell, *Transformations of Myth* I). The moon in bull form, therefore, might be considered both the consort and the son of the goddess. In one wall painting at Çatal Hüyük, a male is actually depicted with bull's horns perhaps indicating his ritual role.

According to Marija Gimbutas, the bull as the moon is part of a cluster of images surrounding the goddess of the Neolithic Era in her role as the goddess of life, death and regeneration. This image-cluster, states Gimbutas, is made up of "symbols of becoming" such as crescents and the horns of the bull which symbolize the waxing and waning aspects of the moon. The bull and moon are clearly the invigorating force of life, and "the worship of the moon and horns is the worship of the creative and fecund powers of nature," both female and male. The role of the goddess is primary in this process, and the role of the bull is essential in both its life-giving and death embracing aspects. Therefore, the bull is represented in sets of four to symbolize the four stages of the moon from the first quarter moon, to the full moon, to the third quarter moon of descending energy and subsequent disappearing, and, finally, to the death of the moon in its new moon phase. Often depicted as four-fold designs on pottery, this abstract symbology presents a continuous striving towards the act of creation from death (*Old Europe* 91).

Gimbutas remarks that "a portrayal of the head of a bull with the lunar disc between its horns occurs in a relief on a vase from a Late Cucuteni site of Podei" with the bull's horns shown upside down in one section of the vase perhaps to symbolize the dead or sacrificed bull. "The Great Goddess," states Gimbutas "emerges from the dead bull in the shape of a bee or butterfly "(*Old Europe* 91). This symbol emphasizing the birth and death process as a continuum with what Gimbutas calls "periodic regeneration" is easily adapted and aptly suited for the process in the heavens where the moon is observed as doing much the same. It is no wonder that The Horns of the Bull or the sacred Horns of Consecration, which resemble the lunar crescents, become important symbols in the Neolithic Era. Hundreds of horned stands with a hole in the center for the insertion of some divine image associated with the goddess of regeneration are found in Vinča and East Balkan civilizations. Gimubtas asserts that they are probably associated with the sacrificed bull's body from which new life emerges in the form of the "epiphany of the Goddess" (*Old Europe* 93).

The "epiphany of the Goddess," continues Gimbutas, takes on many forms in Neolithic culture when shown in conjunction with the horns of the bull or moon. Her epiphany may take the form of the bee and the butterfly, or it may take the form of a flower, a tree, or a column of watery substance. In frescos at Çatal Hüyük, The Goddess and the Bull are also associated with triangles, diamonds, honeycombs, caterpillars, bands or multiple zig-zags (water), hands, brushes, whirls, and eggs, all symbols of becoming and regeneration. On ceramic art, sculptures of bulls or horns, especially in vase painting, are "consistently allied with the energy symbols of snake coils, concentric circles, eggs, cupmarks, antithetic spirals, and life columns." A tiny bull from Bavaria even has four dots on its forehead which are repeated over concentric circles most likely representing the four phases of the moon (*Language of the Goddess* 265–67).

In human terms, the "epiphany of the Goddess" would most likely be equivalent to the resurrection and rebirth of the soul of the individual after death. This would easily explain why The Horns of the Bull are found on or inside many of the megalithic monuments of the Neolithic Era in Western Europe. Gimbutas notes that in the tombs on Sardina which date to the fifth millennium B.C., "Sardinians carved one of the important symbols of regeneration—the bovid head, or bucranium—into many hypogea walls" (*Living Goddesses* 63). The bucrania are found above the tomb's entrance, on both sides of the entrance, or inside the tomb. The idea of regeneration of life or resurrection of the soul is further emphasized by the ochre-red walls of the tomb, symbolizing re-birth from the Mother Goddess, and the decorations on the walls in the tomb that often contain images of regeneration such as double spirals and/or moon cycle symbols (63).

On the entrance to a subterranean tomb of the Ozieri of Sardinia, there are four bull's heads across the top of the entrance to the tomb and one larger bucrania on the side of the entrance (Gimbutas, *Living Goddesses* 36). The four bucrania, like the four bucrania in the temples of Çatal Hüyük and the four-fold designs on the pottery of the other Neolithic peoples, quite possibly represent the four phases of the moon. The larger, fifth head on the side entrance might signify the completion of the process of the moon's precessional cycle. In other words, the moon's orbit around the earth will be in sync with the orbit of the earth around the sun in five years. This coordination of lunar-solar time is often represented by the number five in archeoastronomy where monuments such as Stonehenge accurately record the syncretization of the moon and the sun, an event noticeable and perhaps sacred to the ancients.

In *The Serpent in the Sky: The High Wisdom of Ancient Egypt*, Anthony West remarks that the number five is the number of eternity or the universal number symbolizing reconciliation, "incorporating the principles of polarity in the manifested universe" (52). In this philosophy, the regeneration of the soul might be seen as both an event in the sky and an event in human history where the finite is reconciled with the infinite or the individual is reunited with the goddess and becomes part of eternity through her powers of regeneration. The four directions of the universe and the four phases of the moon are made complete with the addition of the fifth element representing the human transformed into the eternal, or the cycle of birth, death, and rebirth. As a person stands in an ancient monument, the four directions become her vantage point, and she becomes the fifth dimension or the zenith. Hence, the form of the Egyptian pyramids which enable the soul to aspire to the heavens. Whether the Neolithic peoples of Western Europe and the Mediterranean were suggesting this in their bucrania on their tombs is speculative; however, it is quite possible that civilizations such as these were as advanced as the Egyptians when it came to archeoastronomy and the philosophy of the infinite.

The actual process of ascension and the rising of the soul to eternal life are often symbolized by life itself emerging from the horns of the bucrania in Neolithic sculpture and art. Like the epiphany of the goddess, the epiphany of all life depends on the growth cycles represented by the bull or the moon. According to Gimbutas, the process of new life emerging from the bull or the moon is often associated with "cosmogonic primordial waters" of a "taurian nature" where the invocation of a name in Lithuanian such as "Bitinelis (from 'bite, bee') or "Pilvinas (fat drones with a round, drumlike stomach)" invokes the creation of a lake. Gimbutas remarks that: "The names of such bull-lakes are of great semantic interest for the connections they reveal between the bull, the moon, water, drones, peas and snakes." Some small bull figurines were found near the edge or in the middle of water basins with plants and flowers or bees springing from the bull's body. Additionally, the regeneration of life from the bull is represented by the butterfly, an apt symbol of ascension (*Language of the Goddess* 270).

Some confusion as to the actual nature of these symbols emerging from the bull or the sacrificed body of the bull occurs later in history when Porphyry, a philosopher of the Third Century from the Levant, quotes Sophocles as saying: "Moreover, the ancients gave the name of 'Melissae' to the priestesses of Demeter who were initiates of the chthonian goddess; the name 'Melitodes' to Kore (Persephone) herself; the moon (Artemis) too, whose province it was to bring the birth, they called 'Melissa,' because the moon being a bull and its ascension the bull, bees are begotten of bulls. And souls that pass to the earth are bull-begotten" (Ransome 107). Although this statement unknowingly echoes the Neolithic beliefs of regeneration, it was literally interpreted as a swarm of insects appearing from the carcass of the sacrificed bull as a symbol of new life; fortunately, this idea was laid to rest by the mid-nineteenth century, and the idea of "spontaneous generation" is interpreted as dramatic (Gimbutas, *Language of the Goddess* 270).

However, the tradition of strange bee-like creatures or goddesses of a butterfly nature emerging from the sacrificed bull does have a literal and very real basis. Near many slaughterhouses, there is a pond or run-off water source where the blood of the sacrificed bulls drains. On the surface of the water of this blood-pond, bees and butterflies gather to feed on the blood-filled waters. On occasions where the bull has just been sacrificed, the water surface of the pond may be covered with masses of butterflies and bees sustaining themselves on the nourishment of the bull's blood. The entire water surface appears as a pulsating force of new and vibrantly colored life seemingly possible only with the blood of the sacrifice. Interestingly enough, this gives yet another meaning or dimension to Gimbutas' references to the bull ponds or lakes and the association of the bull with water, butterflies, and bees. The bull, bees, and butterflies are also connected, by both Porphyry and Sophocles, with the chthonian goddess, or the goddess of the waters of death, and with the moon goddess, or the goddess of regeneration.

The associations of the bull's heads and the image-clusters of regenerative life forms with emblems such as the bee and butterfly with their "antennae like bull horns and wings in the form of a lunar crescent" become a dominant theme in Neolithic art because of their similar forms (Gimbutas, *Old Europe* 183). However, the images of death such as the vulture or vulture skulls which also appear frequently with bucrania are less similar in schematic form to the bull and the moon. Although they are depicted in many Neolithic temples, the vultures and bird forms appear as separate deities from the image-cluster, yet as a necessary part of the schemata. As an early association of the bird-goddess, the vulture appears on temple murals at Çatal Hüyük in reference to the Neolithic excarnation rites which may or may not be accurate according to recent discoveries. However, according to Melaart, as the giver of life, the goddess as vulture is also the taker of life because she cleaned the dead before the bodies were returned to the family for burial and rebirth (24). Campbell also notes a chapel in Çatal Hüyük where the bull's head as returning moon has a vulture facing it on another wall where the vulture is eating back the head of a headless body as a type of rebirth or recycling of the soul which, according to Campbell, might be construed as being contained in the head. (*Transformations of Myth* I).

Although the majority of the representations of the bull or moon and the goddess of regeneration are in artistic forms, a significant number of representations in the Neolithic Era are abstract symbols depicting the same process of life, death, and re-birth associated with the moon and the passage of time. It is almost as if a symbolic language has been created to express the passage of cyclical time. Gimbutas notes that spirals, circles, coils, crescents, hook, horns, four-corner signs, brushes, combs, hands and feet, and animals with whirls or processions are all symbols of energy and unfolding. Gimbutas continues: "These dynamic symbols are either themselves energy incarnate or are stimulators of the process of becoming. Moving up, down, or in a circle, they symbolize cyclical time. The pulse of life demands an unending stream of vital energy to keep it going" (*Language of the Goddess* 277). Among those mentioned many such as horns, crescents, and the four-corner signs are obviously notations of lunar cycles.

The lunar cycle is represented by a left crescent, a full moon in the center, and a right crescent moon. This symbol used today to indicate the monthly cycle of the moon is an exact representation of the moon as it rises in the east as first quarter moon, becomes full further south, and then sets in the southwest as the third quarter moon each month. As a unit of four, which takes into account the new or dark phase of the moon, the symbols appear as four-corner signs. Crescents and concentric circles on Neolithic pottery and on passage graves are lunar notations indicating the waxing moon, the full moon, the waning moon and the new moon in its four stages, respectively. The bull is represented in this symbolic language in the abstract with a crescent moon as his horns or as a U-sign indicating the bucrania. As mentioned previously, the U-sign for the bucrania is on hypogea and tombs as well as on the pottery.

Perhaps, the most interesting symbol of this language of lunar becoming is what Gimbutas calls "the hands of the Goddess" found on the walls of Neolithic shrines (*Language of the Goddess* 306). At Çatal Hüyük, one panel contains nineteen hands of red and black, which represent the colors of life and death, respectively. As the color white often represents death to the Neolithic peoples, the red and black hands might therefore represent the cycle of death and rebirth specific to The Goddess and the Bull. The hands form two vertical columns and are joined by a honeycomb, the symbol of regeneration associated with bees. In the palm of each hand is a circle or concentric circles with dots or lines in the center of each circle, most likely full moon symbols for different full moons over a period of nineteen years. In another shrine, the same hand motif appears below two bull's heads, each marked with a honeycomb pattern. It is quite possible that the measurement of this nineteen year cycle, where the moon after 235 lunations meets the sun at exactly nineteen solar years, was one of the most important time-keepers of lunar precession for the ancients, especially when the full moon is measured in The Horns of Taurus every year in the night sky.

On the standing stones, mounds and circles found in Europe, there is evidence that the Neolithic culture reached a sophisticated and advanced stage in astronomy. Monuments, passage-graves and stone circles such as those found in France, Germany, Great Britain, and Spain contain ancient calendar notations which represent the cycles of the year as well as the cycles of precession. Moreover, the symbolic language containing notations of astronomy which has been depicted on the walls of shrines and hypogea as well as on the Neolithic pottery at Çatal Hüyük takes a highly sophisticated form on the monuments of the late Neolithic Era in Europe and the British Isles. On the monuments of this culture, such as Stonehenge, the cycles of the moon are clearly indicated as a vital part of the religious life, the language, and the science of an advanced civilization concerned with the passage of time beyond the yearly cycle. The documentation of the luni-solar and stellar precessional cycles through the skies is an attempt on the part of our ancestors to understand the infinite, important enough to them as it could be to us, to carve into the stones of time.

The language of the stones on the ancient monuments in Europe and the British Isles resembles the symbolic language described by Gimbutas as a language with an energy incarnate to stimulate the process of becoming. Although there is a lack of any animal forms, such as the bull and the bee or butterfly, the language itself is a vibrant language created to express the passage of cyclical time as a monumental event. In *The Stones of Time* by Martin Brennan, Brennan observes that: "It is essential to realize that in megalithic art the elements in a composition are frequently different aspects of one thing in the process of change" (156). The position of the designs in the mound and the relative time at which the moon or the sun's rays illuminate the designs brings them to life as a process rather than a static form of symbolic expression.

In the Brú na Bóinne complex of mounds in Ireland, which includes Newgrange, Dowth, and Knowth and the nearby mounds at Loughcrew, the symbolism of the moon is depicted as twelve full moons to represent the yearly cycle using circles and crescents much the same as those depicted at Çatal Hüyük. However, on a stone on the outer circumference of the mound at Knowth (SW22), the intercalary moon is represented in a more complicated pattern than it is represented on the five bucrania at Çatal Hüyük. Here, the pattern of the full moons and crescents has a center wave depicting a five year calendar complete with the intercalary moons in order to balance lunar and solar time, the basis of the calendar of the ancient Celts. On the Knowth stone, according to Brennan, "Each turn of the wavy line represents one month, or a complete circuit of the distinct but related pattern of crescent and circle repeat units which are closely matched to the phases of the moon" (144).

Precessional cycles of the moon engraved on the monuments are as complicated as the circles, crescents, and wavy lines when they represent the cycles of the moon longer than the five year cycle. At the Neolithic mounds of Knowth and Dowth, spirals indicate the way in which sequences are arranged perhaps indicating the unfolding of time, and a cartouche of nineteen lines near a group of arcs and circles indicates the nineteen year cycle of the moon (Brennan 143). At Dowth, one kerbstone charts the series of eclipses in the nineteen year lunar cycle, and the total number of kerbstones around the monument represents the nineteen year cycle (Murphy 1–4). Although the bucrania are not represented in the symbolic language on the stones at the Brú na Bóinne, the symbol of the "U," depicted in sets or four or outlining a set of crescents at Knowth reflects the "inherent symmetry manifested by the moon and the heavens." Brennan believes it may represent "the dome of the heavens," or a figure of the firmament of the heavens hovering over the stones themselves (154).

Both the lunar cycles of precession and the "U" are represented at the Neolithic stone circles in Europe and the British Isles as well as on the mounds. Instead of using symbols and notations to illustrate the astronomy, the stone circles of time are interactive with the elements. The patterns of the moon, sun, and stars are seen through the trilithons or over the site lines of the circles of stones bringing our ancestors an immediate experience with the infinite cycles of time. The sense of becoming an active part of the changing cycles of time by observing the celestial bodies first hand, perhaps in ritual as well as individual use, brought our ancestors a full sensory and intellectual experience with the heavens.

In bringing down the moon, the ancients were also concerned with identifying the lunar cycles of precession caused by the pulls of the moon on the earth by noting what astronomers call "nutation." "The circular path of precession that the celestial pole of the earth traces out on the celestial sphere is not perfectly smooth, but slightly wavy. This irregularity is called "nutation," the result of a regular 'nodding' of the earth's poles towards and away from the ecliptic poles" (Ridpath 43). Lunar nutation is represented on certain of the stone circles; nutation is actually seen where the full moon rises and sets at different declinations over a period of 18.6 years representing the changing position of the moon. Represented on the panel which depicts the nineteen red and black hands, most likely the hands of the goddess, at Çatal Hüyük and on the stones at Knowth in the wavy lines and crescents, the nineteen year cycle and the nutation of the moon are both an important foundation to express the idea of the infinite through the precise. Here, in the stone circles, is where cosmology melds with the symbols of a culture that reveres the moon both in the imagination and in reality. This does not take away from the art and symbolic language of the ancients in their desire to express their awe of the infinite but adds a dimension to it.

The nineteen year cycle and the nutation cycles of the moon recorded at the stone circles expresses the idea of regeneration or periodic growth and a sense of becoming by directly witnessing the powers of regeneration. Like the monthly cycles of the regeneration of the moon, the precessional cycles are part of the lunar wave of eternal undulating energy which all plant and animal life responds to. In a practical sense, the observations of these declinations of the rising and setting of the full moon on the horizon in different positions forming an arc or part of a continuing wave afforded the ancients another calculable way of determining when they would have more moonlight at the winter solstice or how the tides would change over time. In an abstract sense, the chartings of the nineteen year cycle and those of nutation gave them a sense of being part of an infinitely larger cosmos than themselves. Even in a ritual sense, observing the wave of moons over the stones in larger cycles helped them keep track of time in their own lives.

When the builders of Stonehenge began to record the cycles of time in the late Neolithic Era, they started with the lunar notations of the nineteen year cycle and the nutation cycles of the moon. In Stonehenge I, the first circle of holes called the Aubrey Holes, is a circle of 56 holes which represents three nutation cycles of the moon. Perhaps, the circle also represents a full lifetime of an adult, or in the language of the goddess, it may represent the triskele of the maiden, the mother and the crone, three stages of the feminine cycle. The 56 markings in the circle are siting holes on the horizon which may have once held huge posts, perhaps posts which supported a circular platform of wooden lintels used as a level wooden horizon to accurately record the risings and settings of the heavenly bodies (Heath 4). Thus, the ancients would have had a full circle of the horizon for viewing the moon, the stars, the planets and the sun. In other words, the Aubrey Holes may have acted as a full representation of the life cycle on earth and in the heavens.

The Aubrey Holes also act as a luni-solar calendar, another symbol of the circle or wheel of life where the moon and the sun are brought into the same circle and their cycles are charted in corresponding patterns. In this configuration, markers are moved from one hole to another at dawn and dusk to chart the diurnal rhythm of the day/night cycle. According to Heath: "The Sun marker is moved two holes every thirteen days, thus copying the Moon's daily angular motion. The calendar is therefore an 'integrated' soli-lunar calendar, and if the Moon marker is made to skip over the Sun marker at every new Moon, and a further skip forwards is made at the four key points in the year, equinoxes and solstices, an accuracy of 99.9% may be achieved for the Moon, whilst the Sun's accuracy remains at 99.8%" (55). At a glance, the Aubrey Holes depict the current phase of the moon, the current season, and the position of the moon and the sun in the year.

Finally, the Aubrey Holes accurately predict lunar eclipses. By moving marker stones around the 56 Aubrey Holes, one move for each year, the position of the moon in the nineteen year cycle is easily kept track of thereby allowing the ancients to know the most likely time of the year when lunar eclipses occur. Using the Aubrey Holes, a lunar eclipse occurs "about three holes in a clockwise direction from the previous eclipse on one particular side of the circle. Three holes corresponds to nineteen days, and in nineteen years, the cycle of eclipses completes a full circuit" (Heath 57). The symbolic use and the sacredness of the number "nineteen" is both aesthetically pleasing and mathematically accurate. It is no wonder that the Druids when using Stonehenge at a later date in history still sang their sunrise and sunset songs to deify the movements of the moon and the sun while moving a marker around the circle of life.

Almost contemporary with the Aubrey Holes, a ditch and bank with a wide gap in the bank facing the northeast were dug at Stonehenge I in the late Neolithic Era. The ditch and the bank which was originally six feet high would have provided a level horizon in the center of the circle to view the heavenly bodies. From the center of Stonehenge, the gap in the bank subtends an angle of 10 degrees, just covering the arc of the horizon where the moon would appear to rise during one half of the nineteen year cycle (Wood 100). The gap in the bank was once flanked with two large stones, one of which is the Slaughterstone. During this early stage of Stonehenge, a number of post-holes were also discovered around the entrance of the gap in the bank which marks the extreme lunar risings in the nutation cycle of the moon. These post-holes mark the direction of the rising of the midwinter full moon, as seen from the center of the circle, disclosing yet another marking of the worship of the moon in its nutation cycle in the night sky (Wood 101).

Astronomers who have studied Stonehenge from Gerald S. Hawkins and Alexander Thom, to John Edwin Wood and Robin Heath agree that the original Stonehenge was about lunar astronomy and was a lunar observatory from its earliest times. The earliest known observer of this phenomenon was Diodorus Siculus, a Greco-Roman historian writing in the first century B.C, who describes the ancient peoples to the north, called the Hyperboreans.

Diodorus states that these ancient peoples worshipped the god Apollo when Apollo visited the island they inhabited every nineteen years at their "magnificent circular temple adorned with many rich offerings" (Heath 181). Although Diodorus accurately records the observance of the nineteen year cycle of the moon at the circular temple, which is presumably Stonehenge, he might have translated their worship of Apollo as a worship of Apollo and Artemis, the deities of the sun and the moon, respectively, enlivening the discussion to include both the sun and the moon in their corresponding cyclical patterns that are depicted at the circle of the Neolithic peoples.

The observance of the cycles of the precession of the moon is indigenous to the stone circles and circle formations of the Neolithic culture of Europe and the British Isles and not just a phenomenon of Stonehenge I. Of the many circles, standing stones, U-shaped stone formations, and stone rows of the Neolithic culture, there are a dozen or so sites that have been identified as observatories of the lunar cycles beyond the year. Within a few hundred years of building Stonehenge I, the Neolithic peoples built the Dorset Cursus in east Dorset, Britain. The Dorset Cursus is a ceremonial path or enclosure bordered on either side by a low bank and ditch similar to the one on the Avenue of Stonehenge I (Hawkins 78). From the center of the cursus, there is a terminal which is a carefully leveled platform that acts as an observatory for sitings of the moon on the horizon. The cursus provides sightlines for the moon at minor and major standstill points in its nutation cycle (Wood 102).

Further to the south-west of Stonehenge and the Dorset Cursus, on the moors of Dartmoor in Devon, is a stone complex that dates to 3500 B.C. Merrivale, or "the pleasant valley," is a complex of several stone circles, an avenue, a double row, a single row, a cist, standing stones, and hut-circles that formed a Neolithic settlement. The row of standing stones marks the moon's maximum and minimum rising points against the horizon serving as a backsight for the nutation cycle of the moon (Heath 26). At lands-end in Cornwall at the very tip of south-west England, four stone circles, known as Boscawen-Un, Maen yu daus, the Merry Maidens, and Tregeseal East are all circles of nineteen stones that date to the Late Neolithic Era. Boscawen-Un and the Merry Maidens, both with granite stones that face towards the interior of the ring, have legends associated with them about maidens turning to stone as they danced for the full moon ceremonies (Burl 34). These circles, as well as Tregeseal and Maen yu daus, clearly mark the nineteen year cycle of the moon and perhaps served as temples of the moon.

In Scotland, the Stones of Stenness in Orkney or "The Temple of the Moon" and Temple Wood in Kilmartin or "Half Moon Wood" are two Neolithic observatories that are associated with the moon through their popular names. The Standing Stones of Stenness or Temple of the Moon is a Late

Neolithic circle-henge with more impressive and taller stones than the Ring of Brodgar or Temple of the Sun whose stones are visible to the north. At Stenness, the henge's ditch and bank may have risen 6 feet above ground, and the stones themselves stand as tall as 18'6" high. Legend has it that in the time it takes for the moon to travel its path through the night sky, a dance or procession around the stone called the Odin Stone by the Vikings was performed; at nine full moons, the dancers looked through a hole in the Odin Stone hoping for a vision of the future (Burl 148). At Temple Wood or Half Moon Wood, the Kilmartin stones, a small northern ring which began as a timber setting, accurately measures the declinations of the moon in its nutation cycle or journey through the heavens (Wood 109–12).

In addition to the circles and standing stones in the Neolithic complexes, the "U" formation of stones takes a central role in depicting the cycles of the moon. Looking back to the bucrania with their "U" shape and the association of the "U" as part of the lunar wave charted at Knowth, and looking forward to the "U" shape of The Bluestone Ellipse at the center of Stonehenge III that measures the nutation cycle of the moon, the "U" acts as a central image for the moon in many cultures. From the northern islands of Scotland to Central Europe, the image is dominant. For instance, the stones Machrie Moor in Southwest Scotland on the Isle of Arran, are Neolithic monuments consisting of ruined chambered tombs, hut-circles, and megalithic rings erected around two concentric rings of posts with a horseshoe-shaped timber setting at their center (Burl 114–15). Like the horseshoe stones discovered at Carnac and in the Gulf of Morbihan, France, the Machrie Moor horseshoe marks the extreme rising and setting points of the nutation cycle of the moon using the "U" shape.

The Neolithic horseshoes of stone discovered in France are Tossen-Keler on the northwest coast of Brittany, Er-Lannic on the Gulf of Morbihan in Brittany, and Kerlescan West and North at Carnac on the southwest coast of Brittany. At Tossen-Keler, there is a horseshoe-shaped cromlech open to the east with fifty-six stones flanked by two entrance stones. This granite horseshoe that dates back to 3300 B.C., most likely represents the same lunar alignments that the 56 Aubrey Holes mark as the cycles of precession of the moon. The opposing chevrons and the hafted stone axe engraved on three of the stones are similar to the images of regeneration discovered at Çatal Hüyük. Unfortunately, the horseshoe at Er-Lannic in the Gulf of Moriban was partly submerged when the sea level rose in Roman times; however, the stones that are still visible measure the moonsets and moonrises at their most northern positions. There are two horseshoes at Carnac: Kerlescan West is a horseshoe open to the northeast with an avenue of eighteen stones, and Kerlescan North is an enormous horseshoe whose exact number of stones is beyond determining (Burl 251–59).

Although the stones of time speak to us of the patterns of the moon in terms of astronomy and symbology, traces of the ideology represented in the lunar cycles of precession are apparent in later texts that describe the Neolithic peoples and their beliefs. The beginning of what Gimbutas has called the belief in the moon's ability to regenerate life and bring forth life through symbols of becoming is evident in the Irish mythology in the *Lebor na h Uidre, The Book of the Dun Cow*, a surviving manuscript from the Twelfth Century. Here, one of the five holy people mentioned in the "Dinnsenchas" or poems of the sacred places of Ireland, named Tuan, The White Ancient, represents the belief in reincarnation and the regeneration of the spirit. Moreover, Tuan is the memory of learned truth, legend and knowledge. He is the story-bearer who witnesses the conquests of the tribes of Ireland over thousands of years, first as a man and then as a stag, a boar, and a sea-eagle, Lord of the Skies. Finally, he is born as a salmon, eaten by the wife of Cairell, and born again as a man, the son of Cairell, King of Ireland. As a precursor of Taliesin, the Welsh Bard, and Amergin, the Irish bard, Tuan truly represents the ideas of becoming and regeneration. Like the bull and the moon that are born of the goddess, Tuan opens the doors of precession recording the life of our ancestors and regenerating with each cycle of time. As The White Ancient and Lord of the Skies, Tuan embodies the cycles of time.

The myths of life, death and regeneration evolve into an archetype of major importance in the Bronze and Iron Ages of Europe and the Mediterranean. From the Minoan-Mycenaean iconology of The Goddess and the Bull, to the Iron Age Greek and Celtic myths of The Goddess and the Bull, the moon is an ever-present symbol in the process of becoming. Its phases act as a guide throughout the year, and the cycles of precession evident in the five and the nineteen year cycles of the moon, open doors to cycles in our lives and the lives of our ancestors. Again, through the magnificent temples of the ancients, the lunar cycles of precession are experienced as a rejuvenation of spirit which offers glimpses of eternity. From the epiphany of the goddess, the progenitor of birth, and the waxing and waning of the moon as the fecund powers of the bull, the primary masks of our development open the doors of precession.

Chapter Two

The Astronomer Priestesses
of the Bronze Age

In the history of the human imagination, The Bronze Age captures the most vibrant imagery of the moon and its forces of replenishment, vitality and strength. There is evidence that The Bronze Age culture both worshipped and adored the power of humanity when complemented with their carefully charted journeys of the heavenly bodies. In Bronze Age Greece, in the mainland and especially on the island of Crete, the image of the Mother Goddess is deftly connected with the powers of nature, and, in particular, she is associated with the bull as a virile force of fertile rejuvenation of the lunar and solar energies. In the Minoan-Mycenaean cultures of Crete and Mycenae, the Mother Goddess and her adorant, young male consort become clear representatives of the heavens.

The cult of the Mother Goddess and her association with the rejuvenating forces of the moon and the sun as well as her association with the bull, gives rise to a class of exceptional women who were the astronomer priestesses of the Minoan-Mycenaean culture. These priestesses combined the secular with the sacred lines of the religious imagination in a way that most moderns would find quizzical. The differentiation between what is defined as sacred or holy with what is human is absent in this culture. The priestesses are both the reincarnation of the goddess as well as her representatives on earth. Their many aspects also merge to form what is probably one of the few examples of a matri-local religion and mythology where the central figure seems to be an almost monotheistic goddess with her many roles, not singularly defined or personified, but combined to form an all-powerful deity of generous proportion. Unlike many cultures that depict a Mother Goddess in the Neolithic culture who subsequently is divided into many female deities in the later Bronze and Iron Ages, the original Neolithic Mother Goddess on Crete and in

parts of the mainland in Greece reaffirms her monotheistic attributes by retaining an omnipresent presence in both the mythology and in the religious
rituals. Here, she becomes both the progenitor and the priestess: the embodi-
ment of the divine and the earthly as one force with many faces.

The fascination with a figure as dominant as the Mother Goddess of the
Minoan-Mycenaean religion and mythology is enhanced by her connection
with the moon, the bull, and the rejuvenating forces of nature and humanity.
Unlike the European cultures to the north, the Bronze Age Minoans and Minoan-Mycenaeans did not choose to build stone circles representing lunar and
solar cycles. Instead, they choose to build labyrinths into temple-complexes,
peak sanctuaries, and an acropolis to chart the heavens. Artifacts from these
sacred spaces or *temenea* as well as their orientation to the heavens and the
actual robes, crowns, and jewelry worn by the astronomer priestesses attest to
the fact that they were duly attuned as individuals and as a culture to the mo-
tions of the celestial bodies. In particular, they were most interested in when
the moon and the sun come together in the heavens in their cycles. This re-
union of lunar and solar power symbolizes a reincarnation of human energy.
In the intercalary moonth, in the nineteen year cycle, and in the larger cosmic
cycles of the almost full moon when it joins the sun in the heavens, especially
at the solstice where it may be charted in the horns of Taurus or the Bull, they
envisioned a rebirth of energy which could be transferred to the people. As a
sea-faring people, these Bronze Age travelers were interested in keeping time
by the night sky both on land and sea to arrange their lives according to the
cycles of the moon and the sun.

Perhaps the most interesting documentation of the astronomer priestesses
of the Bronze Age is found in the evidence compiled from the excavations of
the temple-complex at Knossos in Crete. The northeast section of the complex, like several important sites on mainland Greece, dates to the Neolithic
Era where the temple was originally built near a sacred freshwater source
with a northeast siting line to the heavens. On mainland Greece, the magnificent temple at Delphi has, at the base of its mountain, a sacred water source
for pilgrims to use as a lustral basin before climbing to the Temple of Apollo,
a temple aligned to the northeast. Below the northeast corner of the Acropolis at Athens, the caves of the Neolithic peoples mark the first habitation at
the site with sixty sacred wells of the Agora close by. At the mountain citadel
of Mycenae, the northeast corner of the great palace was originally the site of
the Neolithic peoples where the Cyclopean Wall guards their sacred water
source and cistern structure. Likewise, the Temple to Poseidon at Sounion and
the Temple to Aphaia on the island of Aegina have fresh water sources and
caves of the Neolithic peoples at their northeast corners.

The significance of the freshwater sources is easily understood considering the dry and dusty climate of the Mediterranean, and the fact that the waters were deemed sacrosanct follows. However, the reason for the alignment of many of these mountain sanctuaries to the northeast may be better understood when compared to the alignment of many other Neolithic structures found in Europe such as Stonehenge, Carnac, and the stone circles in Cornwall and Scotland. The "U" formations at the center of these structures, which measure the nineteen year cycle of the moon in conjunction with the sun, also act as a siting line for the rising of the constellations in the northeast. Each season a set of constellations rises in the northeast identifying the deities of the night sky. To the ancestors, this was the sacred place for the deities to appear to the people and guide them through each agricultural year. Therefore, their myths and rituals follow the patterns of the stars, the moon, and the sun, as their life was based on the deities of the natural cycles of the earth.

At Knossos, the northeast corner of the temple-complex serves as a siting line for the heavenly bodies and a sanctuary for the astronomer priestesses. To enter the temple-complex, the Grand Procession of worshippers followed the Royal Road along the eastern side of the complex, gathering at an open air theatre. In the later Minoan palace excavations, a Lustral Basin area was discovered; it allowed the worshippers to bathe in the sacred water of Knossos which, according to Sir Arthur Evans, in earlier times was actually an open-air spring descending from a height within a walled temenos with its source sheltered by three trees within a line enclosure (III: 138). To approach the farthest point of the northeast section of the complex, one must still travel through a sacred grove of olive trees to the villa of the priestesses. From this corner, a mountain range with a straight line for siting and a niche in the mountain exactly northeast is apparent from its terrace as well as from the upper northeast corner of the Central Court, where rituals and celebrations were held for the people.

In the "Miniature Fresco of the Sacred Grove and Dance," several hundred spectators sit behind three sacred olive trees while the priestesses dance in an open-air arena situated outside the walls of the northeast section of the temple (Evans, III: 67–68). Beyond this scene, past the sacred olive grove and down a small, steep hill are the excavations for the villa of the priestesses. Evans describes his discovery of the villa: "Built into a cutting in the hillside and overlooking the glen of the ancient Kairatos stream, there came to light, about a hundred meters N.N.E. of the North-East Palace Angle, a Minoan house which, though it cannot compare in size with the 'Little Palace' presents a specially elegant aspect in its material and arrangements" (II: 396). Besides the elegant Megaron, the elaborate bathing rooms and the sacrificial

room of the Pillar Crypt, the villa has its own triangular terrace facing the rising stars, sun and moon.

The remarkable layout of the northeast corner of the Knossos temple-complex, which includes the sacred water source of the Neolithic peoples as well
as the open-air dancing floor and terraced villa, is the site for the priestesses
of Knossos to observe the celestial bodies. The other site is far more spectacular than the temple-complex due to its proximity to the heavens. It is the
peak sanctuary of Mt. Juktas, which is west of the Knossos temple-complex.
From the temple at Knossos, the peak sanctuary of Mt. Juktas is aligned to the
center of a massive stone representation of The Horns of Consecration or The
Horns of the Bull. The Horns are aligned southwest, framing the setting sun,
moon, and stars. In a sense, they accent the setting of the heavenly bodies,
whereas the northeast corner, which most probably had similar Horns of Consecration, accents the rising of the same heavenly bodies. From the temple-
complex, the rising and setting of the stars, moon and sun act as demarcations
of the cycles of time and renewal for the people.

To complement the orientation of the Knossos temple-complex, the peak
sanctuary at the top of Mt. Juktas gave the priestesses an optimal place to
view the movements of the celestial bodies with extreme accuracy. Perhaps,
this mountain peak at the top of their world acted as the central position to
site the movements of the heavens without interference, while the temple-
complex itself housed the rituals to celebrate these movements. Excavations
of the priestesses' house, an altar, and a shrine with a another triangular terrace like the triangular terrace at the villa have proven that Mt. Juktas was in
use in the earliest period of the temple-complex culture of Knossos. Furthermore, the triangular terrace of the shrine faces northeast for accurate siting of
the rising of the stars, moon, and sun. Evans describes "what seems to have
been an outer yard or temenos of more or less triangular form, which was supported by rough terrace walls on the immediately adjoining rocky slope to
North and East" of the temple (I: 158).

The excavations of the peak sanctuary at Mt. Juktas also reveal some interesting votive finds that reflect the priestesses' interest in astronomy. Near
the altar, among a variety of votive offerings, a clay sealing with the representation of a bull's head with a star symbol between the horns was discovered (Karetsou 147). A libation table with a ladle at its center, similar to a libation table from the sanctuary at Phaestus with the inscription of 18 bulls
outlining the table, was also discovered at Mt. Juktas. The association of the
bull with the nutation cycle of the moon as well as the association of the bull
with the stars emphasizes the interest that the Minoans had in the larger cycles of time and the movement of the celestial bodies through the heavens.

Evans comments that the shrine on the mountaintop, the sacred peak of the Mother Goddess, is represented most clearly on a gold signet ring from Knossos where she stands on the rocky peak of the mountain ruling the heavens and earth. (I: 159).

Three other gold signet rings, each sized for a woman's small ring finger and each more than likely worn by the High Priestesses of Mycenae, Tiryns, and Knossos include all the aspects of the Mother Goddess and her relationship with the heavens. The three gold rings are clearly symbolic of both the power and influence the priestesses had in the Minoan culture. On the gold ring from the Acropolis at Mycenae, a Minoan pantheon is depicted where the suppliants approach a goddess who is evidently represented by six bull's heads and the Tree of Life. In the celestial sphere above the goddess and her adorants are a moon sickle, a sun, a star disc, and ocean waves in the sky. Likewise, on a gold ring from Tiryns, "the upper part forms a kind of exergue, separated off by an undulating line, and is sprinkled with small dots or points, perhaps meant to represent the stars. In the centre there is a six-spoked wheel, with the spokes projecting a little beyond the ring viz. the sun. On each side there are two boughs and between those on the left of the moon sickle, lying with its horn pointing downwards" (Nilsson 412–13).

The third ring is the famous "Ring of Minos" now displayed in a room of its own in the Museum of Heraklion. Although the ring is identified as the king's ring, it is evident that it is much too small for the hands of a man. The ring, more than likely, belonged to the High Priestess of the temple-complex at Knossos. The subject of the ring is the passage of the Mother Goddess from the Horns of Consecration across the sea and through the olive groves to a sanctuary where she arrives nude with hair flowing and in a perpetual state of ecstasy. A young male greets the goddess on her journey, and a seahorse boat, also with two Horns of Consecration, at the bottom of the ring's surface promises a guided journey. This epiphany of the goddess is a vision of renewal and regeneration complete through the sacred marriage and the Horns of Consecration where the goddess travels through the earth, sea, and air. She ascends to the upper regions as a queen of the heavens and a mistress of the skies. By wearing the rings and participating in the rituals of regeneration, the priestesses were able to transform into the epiphany of the Mother Goddess. All this is carefully charted in the heavens and inscribed in gold.

The priestesses as representatives of the Mother Goddess have several aspects in their iconography that connect them to the practice of astronomy in their rituals. Each aspect, although representative of the powers of the chthonic regions, the earth and the sky, is easily identified in the cycles of the stars, moon and sun. As goddess of the chthonic regions, the Mother Goddess holds snakes and is often seen as the goddess of the House Cult or the protector and sovereign of her region. The constellations that identify her are Ophiuchus, Serpens Caput, and Serpens Cauda or The Serpent Bearer and The Serpents. These constellations dominate the Summer Solstice sky and remain in the sky for the warmer half of the Cretan year. As goddess of the waters and the sea, the Mother Goddess is called Ariadne, Aphaia, or Britomartis and is represented by Corona Borealis, the crown of Ariadne, at the Summer Solstice. As goddess of the earth, the Mother Goddess of the Minoans has two lions or griffins on either side of her and is represented in the heavens as Leo, The Lion, a constellation that rises soon after the Winter Solstice. As goddess of the sky, the Mother Goddess has the aspect of the bull as her consort and son, a symbol of regeneration and fertility and the union or sacred marriage of the moon and the sun; he is represented as Taurus. His cycles are measured when the full moon is in The Horns of Taurus or The Horns of Consecration at the Winter Solstice.

Tracing the corresponding astronomy and iconography of the Mother Goddess in Minoan culture reveals an emphasis in duality and balance in their ideology. In her snake aspect, she holds two snakes on either side of her as she raises her arms high as a symbol of power. Likewise, two lions guard her as earth mother and two griffins sit on either side of her throne in the magnificent fresco of the Throne Room at Knossos. Two bulls are sacrificed to her, and her priestesses as representatives of the goddess hold Double Axes which are often placed in two bucrania for ritual use. More than likely, these Axes were used to measure the cycles of the stars, moon and sun at the two points of balance to the Minoans: the Winter and the Summer Solstice. Like their year, which has two seasons, the Solstices are the two points of reference for the Minoans. The concern with balance and the solstices of the year is evident throughout the Minoan-Mycenaean mythology and cult practices. Perhaps this is a message to keep the perfect balance of nature in the spheres of the Mother Goddess.

Although the aspect of the Mother Goddess most relevant to the study of the moon is her relationship with Taurus, this relationship is not wholly separate and is often better understood, as is the goddess herself, in the context of her diverse attributes. Her association with the chthonic regions and the snake is a vital part of her regenerative strength and her epiphany in the heavens. In a sense, if she is able to rise from the depths of the Underworld and the chthonic regions, which the snake represents, she has achieved the balance of the year traveling through the Winter Solstice and the death of winter to the Summer Solstice with its welcoming rejuvenation. By traversing the year into the larger cycles of time, she is also a symbol of eternal life. The Neolithic symbol for the Snake Goddess is still prevalent in Minoan culture as a spiral or what the Greeks call *oikos*, the center. The *oikos* is a spiral, like the snake, and it symbolizes the coiling and uncoiling of time (Gimbutas, *Old Europe* 94–5).

In the Summer Solstice night sky, the exact stance and posture of the Mother Goddess as seen in the two faience figurines from the Temple Repositories at Knossos is paralleled in the constellations of Ophiuchus, Serpens Caput and Serpens Cauda or The Serpent Bearer and The Serpents. The snakes entwined around the outstretched arms of the goddess and the snake stretching its head towards the top of her tiara are easily identified in the constellations in the outstretched arms that hold the two snakes and in the triangular headpiece, a distinctive mark of the goddess. In this magnificent Summer Solstice view of the constellations all the snakes of the year, including Draco, which was coiled about the North Celestial Pole in the Bronze Age as if it was moving the cosmos itself, emphasize the power and strength of the snake to the ancients.

At Knossos in the North East Hall of the East Wing of the temple complex, snake-coiled, bronze locks were discovered amidst a mass of carbonized wood which was the remains of a large statue of the Mother Goddess. This statue, like the faience figurines of the Mother holding her snakes, is part of what many Minoan-Mycenaean as well as Greek temples called their *xoana* or representations of the ancestors (Evans, III: 522–25). As in the later Greek temples of Athena and Hera, the xoana were brought out to be viewed by the people as a symbol of ancestor worship. At Knossos, the xoana, which was found with an exceptionally large set of Sacral Horns in the North East Hall, is a representative of the goddess as a regenerator of life often depicted with the snakes as her symbol of regeneration. She is the force which brings back the memory of the ancestors and calls on the resurrection of the energy of the snake as a chthonic force. The faience figurines of the Knossos temple-complex, the peoples' most precious xoana, were kept in two large storage chests that were built below the floor and were made of porous stone provided with sheets of lead for protection against the damp (Logiadou-Platonos 64).

Likewise, snakes themselves were kept below the ground in three very large circular pits at the south of the Knossos temple-complex as well as in the temple-complex as house snakes, guardians and protectors of the living and the dead. The pits for the snakes were used as granaries for storage, and the snakes protected the grain from mice or other vermin. As in many ancient cultures, such as the Northern African tribes of the living Neolithic peoples, the snake is contained in the granary to protect the wealth of the tribe in the winter months and uncoiled and freed in the summer months (Griaule 118). Perhaps, the faience figurines are holding the snakes as a symbol of the release of the snake's energy and the energy of the ancestors through their

yearly resurrection. According to Marija Gimbutas: "The mysterious dy-
namism of the snake, its extraordinary vitality and periodic rejuvenation,
must have provoked a powerful emotional response in the Neolithic agricul-
turalists, and the snake was consequently mythologized, attributed with a
power that can move the entire cosmos" (*Old Europe* 94).

On a Linear B Tablet found at the Knossos temple-complex, the name of
the goddess, *po-ti-ni-ja,* is used as a surname or a designated term for the
Mother Goddess; the word translates literally as "Our Lady." To describe her
snake attribute, the word *a-ta-na* is placed before *po-ti-ni-ja* and, according
to Gimbutas, this describes a chthonic goddess that has snake and/or bird attributes such as one goddess with a dove on her head and upraised arms found
in the Hall of the Double Axes (*Living Goddesses* 143–44). These snake and
bird goddesses of the temple-complex often wear a mask with a large nose
and are definitely linked to the Neolithic snake and bird goddesses found in
central Europe, the British Isles, and the rest of the Mediterranean. In the Iron
Age, the Greek goddess, Athena, is the descendent of the snake and bird goddess with the owl and the snake as symbols of this attribute. Miriam Robbins
Dexter notes that "the Linear B syllabary did not indicate aspirated conso-
nants such as the *th*, so *a-ta-na* can indicate Athana, classical Greek Athena"
(*Living Goddesses* 222).

The bird aspect of the Minoan goddess when depicted separately from her
snake aspect is represented as a rejuvenating force of life, a type of Persephone or Kore where her chthonic self takes on a second role in the warmer
months, and she is resurrected from the Underworld as a maiden and bride.
The birds most often associated with her are the dove, the crane, and the peacock. Today, at Knossos, there are still many peacocks at the temple-complex,
and, in the frescos, the priestess and her young male consort wear hats
adorned with peacock feathers. In a fresco entitled "The Prince with the
Lilies" on the western entrance to the Central Court of Knossos, a young male
adorned with peacock feathers enters the ritual space or temenos at the head
of a grand procession for the goddess.

Gimbutas remarks: "In classical antiquity, different names and epithets
identified the same deity in different localities and the Minoan goddess of regeneration too has many names" (*Living Goddesses* 143). As the crane and
bride of Dionysus and Theseus, she is known as Ariadne; on the island of
Aegina off the coast of Athens, she is known as Aphaia, the bride of Zeus; and
as the life-giving force of nature associated with water as an amniotic fluid or
birth-giving source of life, she is Diktynna and Eileithyia. As a bride, she
dances like a bird at her sacred marriage or *hieros gamos* to her young male
consort, and as a maiden, new to womanhood, she is responsible for the

birthing waters of life, the very waters her consort must cross to come to their nuptials.

The hieros gamos of the Minoan goddess in her bird aspect is depicted in later Greek mythology as the marriage of Ariadne to Theseus and the subsequent marriage of Ariadne to Dionysus on the island of Naxos. As in most Greek mythology that depicts Minoan culture, the aim of the myth is to demonstrate the Greeks' dominance over the earlier Mother Goddess culture. Through this screen of unfortunate events, where Ariadne's marriage ends in her abandonment by Theseus, the rituals of the astronomer priestesses are still central. When Dionysus arrives to rescue Ariadne, he consoles her by marrying her and giving her a crown of jewels for eternity in the night sky. This dainty circlet of stars, known as the Corona Borealis or Northern Crown, is the celebrated constellation of the astronomer priestesses at the Summer Solstice where it reaches the zenith in the night sky in close proximity to The Serpent Bearer and The Serpents. Ovid's version describes the constellation: "The wreath flies through the thin air, and as it flies its jewels are turned into fires and become fixed in their place, still with the appearance of a wreath (corona)" (Morford and Lenardon 606).

Where Theseus is a symbol of the cult of the hero, Dionysus is a symbol of the older world order of the Minoan culture. The crown of jewels or Corona Borealis that Dionysus gives Ariadne was used prior to the Greek Iron Age as an important navigational marker to the sea-faring peoples because of its position in the Summer Solstice sky at the zenith. The *hieros gamos* therefore comes to light as a ritual of summer splendor and magnificence for the ancient Minoans through the siting of the constellation. Gimbutas remarks: "The hieros gamos is recognized in the frescoes, gems, and ivory reliefs found in Indo-European, Mycenaean and later Greek art. The repeated theme is that of a bridegroom who comes in his ship from overseas to fulfill the sacred wedding in the sanctuary of the goddess" (*Living Goddesses* 118). The myth of Theseus reverses the action of the bridegroom coming to the temple or sanctuary of the goddess to taking the bride away and abandoning her, a cruel reversal to obviously undermine the power of the goddess and her sanctuary.

Ironically, after Theseus leaves Ariadne and travels to Delos, Theseus and his companions dance the Geranos or Crane Dance, another ritual associated with the hieros gamos of the bird goddess. The dance became traditional at Delos; however, its intricate movements that imitate the windings of the labyrinth were of a much earlier Minoan origin again linked to the astronomer priestesses. Like the hieros gamos itself, whose roots are traced as early as 10,000 BC in the Near East and 5,000 BC in southeastern Europe, the dance has roots in earlier cultures with matri-local traditions (Gimbutas, *Living Goddesses* 18–19). At the center of the labyrinth or angular spiral dancing floor at the Knossos temple-complex is the waxing moon, waning moon or a star; "A similar labyrinth is found on an early seal from the Minoan palace of Haghia Triada, another on a clay tablet from Pylos in the Peloponnesus, and still others on late coins from Knossos from the Classical Greek period, about 350 BC onwards, one with a crescent moon in its centre and one with a rose" (Baring and Cash 135). These symbols of astronomy connect the ritual dance to the heavens.

The dance floor itself is perhaps the most important element found at the Knossos temple-complex that connects the priestesses and their rituals to the hieros gamos of the bird goddess. In the Throne Room frescos, one fresco depicts women dancing in the sacred grove at Knossos (Logiadou-Platonos 54). This fresco entitled, the "Miniature Fresco of the Sacred Grove and Dance," is a depiction of the triangular open-air arena mentioned earlier in its relation to the priestesses' villa on the northeast corner of the temple-complex. It is here, quite possibly, that most of the dance ritual of the priestesses' Geranos or Crane Dance of the Labyrinth took place; "Homer makes a suggestive link between dancing and the labyrinth in his image of Ariadne's dancing floor at the Palace of Knossos, for, as the daughter of King Minos and Queen Pasiphae in the later Greek story, she would have been the high priestess who conducted the ceremonies" (Baring and Cash 135). In performances of living myth, the priestess acts out the epiphany of the goddess becoming the representation of the goddess on earth, a prevalent theme on Minoan signet rings and in the Minoan frescoes.

On a signet ring found in the Tomb at Isopata near Knossos, four female figures engage in a ritual dance in a field of lilies. They have the classic flowing hair and the flounced dresses characteristic of the dancers in the frescoes. All raise their arms in exaltation to greet the figure of the goddess or the high priestess, which descends from the celestial realms through the wavy lines, perhaps designating the passing from one sphere to another, to her adorants; these wavy lines, remarks Evans, "delimit earth and sky, leaving a reserved space for the divinity or the heavenly luminaries." Here, the goddess descends in "a rapid approach from her celestial realm" to become one of the dancers (Evans, III: 68).

In a terra-cotta group of dancing priestesses found at Palaikastro, the dancers form a circle to do a type of ring or chain dance. In this figurine, a dove takes the place of one of the women. These dancers, like the dancers in the frescos and on the signet rings, are part of the aspect of the bird goddess that incorporates both the image of the goddess as bride and bird dancing at her own wedding ceremony. Evans remarks that even today in Crete the dance for the bride is the opening dance at weddings performed by women alone, the bride leading (III: 76). In her bride aspect, the goddess is also married to Zeus as Aphaia on the island of Aegina. This temple, like other ancient temples aligned to the northeast, has the caves of the Neolithic peoples at its northeast corner where a fresh water spring is found.

Aphaia, like Ariadne, is a Minoan goddess who flees from her pursuant Zeus to escape being his bride. Like the Iron Age story of Theseus and Ariadne, Aphaia's marriage ends in tragedy; she is turned into a net and drowned and then Artemis rescues her and gives her immortality. At the site of Aphaia's temple, a column with a sphinx at the top was erected to honor her at the northeast corner next to the sacred water of the cistern. A pediment on the front of the temple, near the sphinx, depicts Aphaia fleeing Zeus. Although Aphaia retains the wings of the bird goddess in the iconography of the sphinx, which has the head of the goddess, the body of the lion and the wings of the bird, she comes to a dreadful end in her unfortunate wooing and does not experience the epiphany of the goddess in the hieros gamos of Bronze Age mythology. Her temple is interesting because it has many of the characteristics of the Minoan goddess and the astronomer priestesses and their temples. The sacred water source, the northeast alignment of the temple, and the large area in front of the temple with Aphaia'a sphinx are all indicative of the temple-complexes of the Minoans. Perhaps the open area in the front of Aphaia's temple was her dancing floor for the celebrations of the stars, the moon, and the sun.

As Britomartis, Dikytnna and Eileithyia, the goddess is represented by a net associated with the life-giving water of amniotic fluid or of childbirth itself as well as the above mentioned association of the goddess as the bride. It seems that both these connotations of the aspect of the Mother Goddess are symbolic of the stage of femininity understood as young womanhood. Here, the maiden comes to fruition as a part of the culture in her ability to actively take part in fertility and creation. She has an active role in the rituals of the astronomer priestesses as an earthly representation of the goddess through ritual as bearer of the sacred waters of life. The constellation that represents the net is The Water Carrier or Aquarius, a late rising constellation in the summer sky. The celebrations to this aspect of the goddess most likely took place in late summer because it is an appropriate time to bring the marriage to fruition. The marriage realized naturally would lead to a celebration of the new life it bears, bringing the life-giving forces of the feminine to a powerful forefront in myth, ritual, and in the night sky.

The artifacts and temples of the Minoan culture stress an obvious importance on the figure of the water-bearer in ritual. The abundance of rhytons used to pour libations for ritual use and lustral basins at the temples attest to the importance of deeming water sacrosanct. A glorious representation of this concept is transformed into art in an excellent rhyton made of rock crystal decorated with gilded ivory and beads from the Palace at Zakros (Logiadou-Platonos 17). Likewise, at the head of the Procession Fresco at the Knossos temple-complex, is a priestess with an aquamarine rhyton; she is called the Cup Bearer (Logiadou-Platonos 49). In the temple-complex at Knossos, other than the lustral basins at the northeast entrance that are a welcome sight to the Grand Procession of worshippers arriving at the temple for cleansing, and other than the sacred waters of the stream of Kairatos through the olive grove at the northeast corner, are spectacular rooms inside the temple known as the "Queen's Megaron." Here, a dolphin fresco adorns the walls and sacred columns decorate the interior, emphasizing the importance of water as a source of feminine energy for the priestesses.

In Greek mythology, the Cup Bearer is Ganymedes, a young man and lover of Zeus (Graves, I: 117). Although Ganymedes or Aquarius is transformed into a young, effeminate male in the Iron Age, in the mythology of the Bronze Age, the Cup Bearer interestingly enough is a feminine force that bears the waters of life in her net. As Britomartis and Dictynna, she is a "Sweet Virgin" or "Sweet Maid" in Linear B of the Mycenaean script. She is said to have escaped her pursuer, who was named Minos in later Greek mythology, to fall into a net in the sea; hence her name translates from the Greek *diktyon* as "net." She is mentioned in an oath of the Knossians and Drerians, and a xoanon wrought by Daedalus was used in her festival representing her as the bride (Nilsson 510). Finally, as Eileithyia, she is represented as the goddess of childbirth in its pure form: the midwife. Her name is associated with the cave of Amnissos on Crete where the goddess gave birth to her young son (Gimbutas, *Living Goddesses* 143).

As Mother Goddess of the forces of the earth, the goddess has two protective griffins or lions on either side of her, or she is transformed into the sphinx as guardian. On either side of her throne in the Throne Room at the Knossos temple-complex are two magnificent griffins in a fresco, and at the gates of the temple-complex at Mycenae, two lions are carved in the massive stone entrance to the temple. At Knossos, the sphinx is a female xoanon of considerable size. These temple animals, whether real or imagined, reflect the Mother Goddess' epiphany where her animal energies are fused with divine energy for transformation and resurrection. Drawing from the earth, the Mother surrounds herself with the beasts of the earth for protection and power. In a Knossian seal called the "Mother of the Mountains," the goddess is on a mountain top with two lions resting their forelegs midway up the side of the mountain.

The meaning of the lion aspect of the Mother Goddess is revealed in the later Greek mythology which is heavily influenced by the Indo-European degeneration of the Old European goddesses. Here, the lion as the Nemean Lion is depicted as the one of the many monsters born of the dreadful Titans, Echidne and Typhon. The powerful couplings of these primordial forces in the creation myths of the Greeks are symbolic of the transformation of the feminine forces of the culture of the Mother Goddess, such as Echidne and her children, into monsters in the eyes of the newly born patriarchy. In the case of Echidne, her incestuous child, the Nemean Lion, represents that power of the Mother Goddess inherent in the earlier Bronze Age cultures that has been transformed into a fearful beast that must be killed by the Iron Age hero, Hercules and worn by him as a symbol of strength. To both the Iron Age peoples and their predecessors, the Lion is found in the night sky as a guiding force of strength during the colder months. The constellation in the night sky that represents this power rises soon after the Winter Solstice and is known as Leo, the Nemean lion, with the primary star of Regulus as its heart.

On the "Ring of Nestor," there are four delimiting spaces belonging to terrestrial spheres with the world tree at the center; each of the four spheres contains images of lions or griffins as well as adorants of the goddess both male and female. In the upper right hand sphere, a lion is adored by two priestesses, and in the lower right hand sphere, three priestesses have griffin heads while another approaches a griffin on an altar. In the left spheres, male and female adorants dance with a griffin-headed priestess or sit with upraised arms in a sacred posture. Apparently, the adoration of the beasts has allowed some to transform into beasts and others to experience transformation indicated by chrysalises and butterflies above their heads and their expressions of joy. This sacred ring, worn by the priestesses, is a pictorial representation of the epiphany of the people through their access with the earth, represented as the tree, the lion, the griffins, and the chrysalises and butterflies. Here, notes Evans, "the sacred Lion of the Goddess is seen in an attitude of vigilant repose" (III: 154).

The griffins and the sphinx, mythical beasts associated with the goddess in the Minoan-Mycenaean culture, are depicted in the Knossian fresco of the Throne Room in vivid colors and on a gem from the cave of Psychro. On the gem from Psychro, two griffins stand attentively on either side of the goddess in another demonstration of her state of exaltation or epiphany. In this representation, the goddess raises her two hands to support three wavy lines above where her head would be; her head is diminutive, almost non-existent. Other gems and rings found with similar depictions of the goddess with lions or griffins on either side of her show the same diminutive head with similar lines. Here, the epiphany of the goddess is depicted as an abstract freeing from one's personage to the energies of the earth. Like the priestesses whose heads are replaced by the head of the griffin in the "Ring of Nestor," fusing of the divine with the earthly forces is seen as a positive transformation for the deity.

The fusion of the earthly beast with the divine is most aptly represented in the figure of the sphinx. As a crystallized form of the epiphany of the goddess, the sphinx is depicted in a sedate manner, both regal and divine. In the Minoan temples, she is a symbol of the overpowering feminine force of the knowledge of the goddess. It is highly probable that a sphinx atop a column might have been situated on the northeast corner of the Knossos temple-complex as a signal to the people of the inherent possibilities achievable through the forces of the goddess. As a beacon, guardian, and crystallized form, the sphinx is the ultimate culmination of the temple animals. She has the crown of peacock feathers of the goddess, the breasts and face of the goddess, the wings of a bird, the body of a lion, and the tail of a snake. In astronomy, she is the center of the sky, the entity on the column of the world axis. Her form exudes the ecstasy of the composite energies of the earth in perfect harmony on the axis of the world tree: a true vision of the imagination in perfect repose.

In the Knossos temple-complex, the remains of what was a xoanon of the Minoan sphinx were found in the drain-shaft deposits of the Treasury Chamber. The xoanon was probably ten or eleven feet in height with a tiara or crown; she was made from the great native cypresses that provided the beams and columns of the temple itself. She had eyes of crystal, brilliant polychrome on her limbs and robes, and various inlays of gold, bronze and gems on her body (III: 525). Her spectacular presence must have overwhelmed the temple inhabitants with awe. A fragment of a fresco of a sphinx was discovered at Knossos with the head of a goddess and a frieze below it of alternating blue and white rosettes. Sphinxes also decorated mirror handles, ivory combs, glass plaques, and other accoutrements of the temple priestesses. The sphinx became as important a figure to the Minoans as it was to the Hittites, Babylonians, Egyptians, and Greeks.

Like the Nemean Lion, the Sphinx of Greek mythology was the child born of incest from Echidne and her son, Orthus. This goddess, like the other children of Echidne, was a man-eating monster who held the secret of the knowledge of man's existence. The Sphinx at Thebes that Oedipus encounters is on a column as the keeper of this knowledge. She too retains the female form of the earlier Minoan-Mycenaean sphinx with the added monster qualities characteristic of Iron Age mythology. She asks Oedipus the riddle of existence and on his correct response, she must submit to him and destroy herself; she throws herself off the Theban acropolis. Although the Sphinx comes to an untimely end, her image is retained in several Greek temples as a footnote to her former powers. She is atop a column in the front of the Temple of Delphi; she is in repose in various forms at Aphrodite's temple at Corinth; and, of course, she still sits high above the temple at the northeast corner of the Temple to Aphaia on Aegina.

Chapter Three

The Goddess and the Bull

The attribute of the Mother Goddess that is most relevant to the study of the astronomer priestesses of the Minoan-Mycenaean culture is the attribute of the bull. The bull as the consort of the goddess is a vehicle for the rejuvenation of the larger cycles of time, those cycles of the moon and the sun that go beyond the rituals and corresponding astronomy of the time-keepers of the year. This resurrection of power and energy lies in the power of The Goddess and the Bull. As a focal point for Minoan-Mycenaean mythology and culture, the bull is represented in The Horns of Consecration, in the sacred bucrania, on rhytons, in The Double Axe of the Minoan astronomer priestesses, in the priestesses' attire, and on the game boards of the Knossos temple-complex. The Goddess and the Bull is therefore an omnipresence force to the people pervading all parts of the spiritual and physical life of the worshippers in order to resurrect the life of the culture.

The priestesses, as the epiphany of the goddess, have the iconology of regeneration in their attire and in their jewelry. From head to toe, they are decorated with what Marija Gimbutas calls "the symbols of becoming," or the symbols of the power of regeneration and birth (*Old Europe* 91). This epiphany of the goddess takes many forms, from butterfly to bee, all dependent on her association with the bull as the fertile, masculine force of the Taurean Age. In a fresco from the Knossos temple-complex depicting a view of the Grand Stand and Spectators, there are nineteen priestesses seemingly about to perform a ritual in the center of the courtyard (Evans III: 47). Whether this is a coincidence that the number of priestesses is the same as the nineteen year cycle of the moon is speculative. However, evidence from Grave Circle A, the priestesses' grave circle at Mycenae, also points to a possible association with the precessional cycle of the moon where there are nineteen shaft graves with fifteen kilos of gold jewelry and gold artifacts. Coincidence or not, both sets of nineteen priestesses at Knossos and nineteen priestesses and their consorts at Mycenae, illuminate the power, flourish, and splendor of a large group representing the Mother Goddess.

In their festive attire, both at Knossos and Mycenae, the priestesses evidently exude feminine power and magnificence as the central focus of their religious spectacles. A passage from Sir Arthur Evans describes the priestesses' attire in the Grand Stand Fresco at Knossos as such:

> We are very far from the restrained pose of Classical Greece. At a glance we recognize Court ladies in elaborate toilet. They are fresh from the coiffeur's hand with hair *frisé* and curled about the head and shoulders; it is confined by a band over the forehead and falls down the back in long separate tresses, twisted round with strings of beads and jewels. In some cases the locks above the forehead curve down in a curious way above the shoulder. The sleeves are puffed, and the constricted girdles and flounced skirts equally recall quite modern fashions. A narrow band appears across the chest, which suggests a diaphanous chemise, but the nipples of the breasts indicated beneath these—in one case the pendent breasts themselves—give a *décolleté* effect. The dresses are gaily colored with bands of blue, red, and yellow, showing white stripes and at times black striations indicative of reticulated and scaled designs like those of the Processional Fresco. (III: 49)

Although Evans' description seems dated, especially in his reference to the priestesses as "Court ladies," his careful attention to detail enhances the overall image of this feminine ritual.

The priestesses' attire when examined even closer reveals an obvious connection to the bull in certain ritual ornamentations. There are several variations in the headdress worn by the priestesses, The Horns of Consecration being but one of them. As the snake aspect of the Mother Goddess, the priestesses wear a high cap accentuated with a coiled snake, and as dancers they wear headbands with jewels resembling the stars at night in their dark tresses. Some wear caps with three poppies in front, while others don similar headbands. The bull aspect of the Mother Goddess is represented by those Knossos priestesses who wear The Horns of Consecration either alone or with birds on either side of the horns (Sakellarakis 91, 95). Where The Horns of the Bull face opposite directions, they symbolize the waxing and waning of the moon from descension into darkness to ascension from that darkness or death to new life.

The resurrection of life from death symbolized by The Horns of Consecration on the priestesses' headdresses is complemented by a type of headdress that uses the crescent moon as a stylized cap sitting toward the back of the head, almost as if it is an early Bronze Age crown. These early crowns use the crescent moon as a cap where the points of the moon rest above the ears giving the appearance of a nimbus or halo behind the priestess' head. Terracotta idols with the crescent moon headdresses were found at Knossos as well as on the acropolis at Mycenae, Aegina, and Athens. In the Acropolis Museum at Athens, the terracotta Bronze Age idols wear crescent moon headdresses painted red or black, the colors of life and death in the iconology of The Goddess and the Bull. Two or three rows of braided hair, resembling snake coils, seem to hold the crescent moon in place. Some of the idols hold a pomegranate or fruit offering to the goddess while others are seated as if on a throne.

In the Iron Age representations and mythology of the goddess Hera, who is associated with the bovine, Hera wears a crown that is of the crescent moon type. She, too, is often seated in her role as Queen of the Heavens and wife of Zeus. Her bovine associations and her crescent crown serve as evidence that she might have been related to the Bronze Age terracotta idols of the Mother Goddess with her bull aspect. Hera retains her association with the celestial realms in Greek mythology as she is the goddess of the year; she was nursed by the Seasons, and she was sought out to be courted by Zeus at Knossos (Graves, I: 50). Once courted, or conquered, this Minoan affiliated goddess gives her powers to the patriarchy and is named Hera from the Indo-European word for year, *yera*. Each year at the Winter Solstice, Hera marries Zeus. In Greek mythology such a powerful deity as Hera retains other aspects, such as the snake aspect and the bird aspect, of the Mother Goddess as well as her association with the heavens and the bull.

Although the crowns of the priestesses at Mycenae from the nineteen shaft graves at Grave Circle A are not the crescent moon headdresses of the Minoan priestesses, they are decorated with lunar configurations. This grave circle of priestesses which dates to the Sixteenth Century B.C. contains the graves of women who were evidently of high stature indicated by the crowns and the gold ritual objects found with them. Seven crowns or diadems, one significantly larger and more decorative than the others, were discovered. These gold elliptical diadems have elongated triangular points decorated with moons and celestial orbs on embossed gold. Each diadem is of fine sheet metal with a repoussé design decorated with moons and what might be considered planets because of the rings surrounding some of the discs. The large crown, presumably of the High Priestess, has three sets of nineteen celestial orbs emblazoned in the finest gold.

Among the Mycenaean priestesses' treasures were sacral knots of amber, triton horns for summoning deities, and an array of crystal and gold artifacts. To further emphasize the regal and celestial powers of the priestesses, the priestesses' graves also contained nine bull's heads in gold cut outs with the Double Axe in the center of each bull's horns. One of the most famous artifacts from Grave Circle A at Mycenae is a massive black bull's head rhyton with gold horns, a gold nose, and gold eyes; in the center of his forehead is a fine rosetta of gold. This rhyton was used in rituals where the libation was poured into the rhyton and released through a hole in the bull's mouth. The liquid of the rituals might have been the blood of the bull as many of the depictions of the bull sacrifice demonstrate the suppliants capturing the blood of the bull as it was sacrificed. A similar bull's head rhyton was found at Knossos where similar rituals were performed. Its horns are also of gold, but it does not have a rosetta on its forehead.

The discovery at Mycenae of a second grave circle, called Grave Circle B, revealed five additional priestesses' diadems with celestial orbs and moons on them. With these diadems were a seal stone with a bull representation and a bull's head with a gold horns and a rosetta on its forehead. It is clear from the discoveries at Mycenae that a cult of Minoan-Mycenaean priestesses dominated the temple-complex during the Bronze Age disappearing with the rise of the Mycenaean kings of the Iron Age. The tragedy of these priestesses and their demise is depicted eloquently in Aeschylus' play entitled *Agamemnon* where Clytemnestra, the wife of Agamemnon is buried at Mycenae with her husband's mistress, Cassandra and Cassandra's two small children. The grave circles at Mycenae are the historical parallel to the tragedy in the sense that they too represent the end of the Bronze Age and the burial of the priestesses and their consorts of the Bronze Age culture. Although the artifacts and actual graves pre-date the play by at least three hundred years, Aeschylus' play symbolizes the advent in history by focusing on one king and his two wives both of whom were evidently priestesses and of high stature in a changing culture. Even though archeologists have deemed that the small gold mask of Agamemnon found in Grave Circle A with the priestesses' crowns is not the mask of Agamemnon, it is a symbol of the lost culture as are the gold masks and body coverings of the two children, possibly dedicated to the children of Cassandra.

Other than the spectacular diadems of the Minoan-Mycenaean priestesses, the priestesses' jewelry and robes reflects an emphasis on the celestial and the adoration of the bull in the Bronze Age cults of the Mother Goddess. Among the jewelry found at the tholos tombs of the Messara Valley and from Mokhlos in eastern Crete, a beaded necklace with a bull's head and three white moons of rock crystal in the center was discovered (Lagiadou-Platonos 12). In the representations of the High Priestess as the Mother Goddess in the Procession Fresco at the Knossos temple-complex and in the representations of the other priestesses at the complex, patterns on the robes of the priestesses are celestial. Embroidered bands on the High Priestess' robe are exceptionally rich in ornament both in the front of her robe and on the borders. The pattern on the hemline border of her robe has three bands of lunar configurations; two bands have blue "U" configurations surrounded by yellow moons while the other band has a series of shaded moons in sequence (Evans II: 609). Reminiscent of the "U" configurations found in Neolithic and Bronze Age cultures, these "U" configurations most likely represent the nineteen year cycle of The Goddess and the Bull as the moon.

The embroidered pattern on the front border of the High Priestess' robe has a large bull's head surrounded by two female sphinxes. On either side of the bull's head and the sphinxes are crescent moons, full moons, and moons divided into sections. Evans suggests that this robe is the "holy robe" of the High Priestess as the epiphany of the Goddess (III: 42). The pattern is distinct because here the bull has eight horns, perhaps symbolic of the rejuvenation of the sun as eight is a solar number representing the solstices, the equinoxes, and the four cross-quarter days of the solar wheel. In the nineteen year cycle of the moon, the moon appears in The Horns of Taurus at the Winter Solstice, one of the eight solar days, and it is here where the two cycles, lunar and solar, combine for their most powerful regeneration or beginning of a new nineteen year cycle. Perhaps the power of the High Priestess comes from this important point of regeneration most aptly symbolized in her epiphany and on her robe.

Star configurations appear in several ancient cultures similar to the star configurations that appear in the Minoan-Mycenaean culture on the robes of the priestesses. In the depictions of the Egyptian Hathor as the moon-cow, stars in the shape of four-pointed crosses are arranged on the bovine form of her body. Evans notes that the exact same star patterns are depicted on the ceiling of Amenemhêt in Egypt as well as on the ceiling at the Knossos temple-complex, and most notably, on the flounced dresses of priestesses in a fresco from Ayia Triada (III: 733). These star configurations are patterned together so as to appear as an infinite series of energy waves over a surface background of midnight blue, representing the infinite energy of the stars. Evans calls this an "Egypto-Minoan" pattern; however, the pattern is also found on the dresses of the statues who might have been the priestesses of Athena in the Acropolis Museum. Here, the stars are red on a background of black, and they cover the priestesses' *chiton* or robe under her cape. On these *kore* from the Archaic Period, the Cretan colors of red and black are displayed as well as the meanders of the labyrinth design and the star configurations from Knossos and Egypt.

Harkening back to the figure of the High Priestess with her crescent moon diadem, where she sits on a throne in the same posture as Hera on her sovereign throne, the Throne Room at Knossos may be viewed as a coherent whole of the many images of the astronomy priestesses present in the culture. On either side of the Throne of the High Priestess are griffins surrounding the throne in much the same posture they surround the bull and the moons on the embroidery of the High Priestess' robe, indicating the role of the priestess as goddess of regeneration. The full moon itself is on the base of her throne, and her lustral basin to perform the rituals of purification and regeneration is not far from her throne in the Throne Room. If wearing her crown and robes, she would have had lunar symbols and symbols of the bull decorating her person as well as jewelry to accent her overall image's connection to the celestial forces. Finally, her ring itself, whether it was the Ring of Minos or several other representations of her epiphany common to the signet rings of the culture, would be the epitome of her power.

A signet ring with just such a scene from the temple-complex at Knossos, reveals the High Priestess on her throne receiving an offering of a libation urn with a full moon suspended above it as if to evoke the lunar powers of the Mother Goddess (Evans IV: 395). The evocation of the Mother Goddess was no doubt part of the stance affected by the priestesses at Knossos where their arms are raised in the configuration of The Horns of Consecration. Several such figures from Knossos are described as evoking a prayer, a benediction, and a gesture "typique de la déesse au moment de son apparition" (Sakellarakis 91). Here, the High Priestess might have offered prayers by raising her arms to form the two crescents of the waxing and waning moon, the crescents of the bull's horns in reverence to the Goddess. If this image were projected into the night sky, Cassiopeia, the constellation that circumnavigates the celestial North Pole and is seen throughout the year as a dominant mother figure, might have been one symbol of the Mother Goddess in the sky. Her stance, like the stance of the priestesses at the Knossos temple-complex, is one of reverence and awe.

The reverence to the bull as a part of the priestesses' rituals and as a symbol of the dying and resurrecting energies of life is depicted in the bucrania, in The Horns of Consecration, in the use of The Double Axe, and on the game boards of the Minoan-Mycenaean culture. The earliest bucrania used with the axe in the priestesses' rituals was discovered in a votive deposit at Mochlos that dates to the Chalcolithic Era and is what Evans calls "the precursor of the 'Horns of Consecration'" (I: 57). At the Knossos temple-complex bucrania are used for both ritual and time-keeping purposes. Bucrania in the anteroom of the Pillar Crypt near the Throne Room and in the Shrine of The Double Axes are ritual ornaments near sacrificial altars. Smaller representations of bucrania are also found on numerous artifacts from Knossos where they decorate altars and miniature temples. In the peak sanctuaries and in the cave sanctuaries, bucrania have also been found near altars or decorating altars for ritual purposes. However, on the outside of the Knossos temple-complex, bucrania are also used as time-keepers of the celestial bodies.

When The Horns of Consecration are situated on the outside of the Knossos temple-complex, their pragmatic significance becomes evident. The Horns of Consecration when facing the northeast measure the rising moon and the full moon in The Horns of Taurus at the Winter Solstice as well as the rising of the constellations each season. Facing southwest, The Horns measure the setting sun and the setting constellations at the Winter Solstice. According to Alan Butler in *The Bronze Age Computer Disc*, Butler states: "The excavations conducted by Sir Arthur Evans indicated that sacred horns adorned parts of the roof lines, and provided they were located at appropriate places (for example, if they fringed the eastern and western flanks of the palace) they may have been used for solar observation." Butler briefly alludes to the fact that The Horns may also measure the constellations and the moon when the celestial bodies fit neatly between them (164). The Minoan astronomer priestesses most likely used The Horns in the same way the Neolithic peoples used the stones, such as those at Stonehenge and the stone circles, to measure the heavens and determine when their holy days and holidays occur.

The measurement of the full moon in The Horns of Consecration at the Winter Solstice is important because this is close to where the galactic equator meets the ecliptic. The galactic equator is the great cosmic circle in the sky that closely follows the Milky Way. The ecliptic or the path of the sun intersects with the galactic equator just outside the end of The Horns of the Bull. When the full moon is at the intersection of the galactic equator and the ecliptic, it is close to where the sun has moved to its lowest place in the underworld at the southern intersection of the galactic equator and the ecliptic, thus signifying its journey into death. Like the moon in its darkest phase, the sun has reached the depths of the underworld below the horizon and is now ready to resurrect into a new life and rise again for a new cycle. At this time, the full moon is clearly on its way to full through the center of The Horns of Consecration where it was exactly nineteen years ago. Both heavenly bodies are undergoing a transformation to begin a new cycle and signal the earth and its people for a resurrection of energy and new life. It is here where the goddess uses the energy of Taurus the Bull to renew herself.

With The Horns of Consecrations as guides, the astronomer priestesses were able to measure the darkest sun turning towards more light at the Winter Solstice of each year in the nineteen year cycle by siting the moon's movements from the Pleiades to Aldebaran. These two points or extremes of the moon's cycle close to the Winter Solstice represent the furthest standstill points of the moon on the horizon; on the stones of the Neolithic peoples, these points are measured by the stones in the "U" configuration often found at the center of the stone circle, as the "U" configuration is at the center of the

concentric circles of Stonehenge. On The Horns of Consecration these two
points are the points of The Horns of the Bull. The moon moves the furthest
north over the Pleiades as a major standstill, and the furthest south over Aldebaran as a minor standstill; this is measured by the left and right points of The
Horns, respectively. When the moon goes through the middle of The Horns
of the Bull, it is going to rise with the sun going down in an eclipse, a dramatic effect for the ancients.

In the Knossos temple-complex, The Horns of Consecration seem to be in
places of high significance in the priestesses' ritual sacred space or *temenos*,
thus connecting their outside purposes of determining the time of the ritual
with their presence at the actual occurrence of the ritual. At the Winter Solstice, the moon's position to the stars tells the priestesses at what point of renewal they are in the cycles of the moon and sun. Logically, these would be
times for sacrifice and resurrection through the giving of animal blood back
to the earth's forces for renewal. Here, the cycle is represented by the bucrania inside or near the Pillar Crypts of the Knossos temple-complex. In the anteroom of the Pillar Crypt near the Throne Room where the xoana of the
snake goddesses of the chthonic regions were kept, Evans remarks that Sacral
Horns of "exceptional dimension" are found (III: 525). Likewise, two pairs of
Horns were found *in situ* in the Shrine of The Double Axes with cult imple-
ments; this section of the temple-complex obviously contained the priestesses' chambers with extravagant apartments, lustral basins, and altars for
sacrifice.

The Horns of Consecration with their twofold purpose, to both measure
and represent the renewal of the goddess with the sacrifice of the bull, are
then positioned both outside and inside the temple at strategic places. The
largest and most magnificent Horns of Consecration greet pilgrims as they
enter the temple-complex on the Royal Road, and Horns of Consecration
framing Mt. Juktas to the southwest still stand to amaze visitors today with
their colossal size. In the restoration of the Central Court of the Knossos temple-complex, The Horns of Consecrations are also set up on the roof of the
entrance porch to denote the sacred character of the building (Nilsson
184–185). Discoveries of The Horns of Consecration on miniature temples at
Knossos and Mycenae also attest to the significance of the bucrania and their
positions at the temples. Finally, the bucrania found in the caves of Mt. Ida
and Mt. Dicte, where the consort of the goddess is said to have been born in
the cave, are noted as bucrania associated with the birthing of the cycle of the
bull or the beginning of the cycle of the moon and the sun as well as those already mentioned in reference to the bull's sacrificial death.

In the cycles of the moon and the sun, the birth and death of each new cycle is heralded with the birth and death of the bull. The bull's association with

the goddess at the beginning, middle, and end of these continuous cycles is measured with amazing accuracy by the astronomer priestesses; however, these occurrences might be viewed as points of delineation in the relationship between the goddess and her consort. What Sir Arthur Evans calls "bull-grappling" are the events that symbolize the sacral nature of the relationship of the goddess and the bull in an active and physically stimulating sense. These events draw the participants and spectators into the living energy that is exchanged between animal and human; in this sense they are earth oriented. Other than the famous bull-jumping depicted in the frescoes of the Minoans, bull-grappling illustrates that vibrant energy the people of the culture express as a vital part of their relationship with their deities. Unlike bull-jumping, which was a magnificent sport for the young Minoan women and men, bull-grappling involves the priestesses and their intimate relationships with the bull.

Bull-grappling took place at the northeast corner of the Knossos temple-complex in the sacred grove of olive trees. Nilsson suggests that the ancient practice of nailing the skull of the sacrificed bull to the sacred tree, or the tree that represents the World Tree with its branches in the heavens and its roots in the underworld, is a precursor of the decorative bucrania on the temples of the Minoans at Knossos and Mycenae (232). It is here, therefore, that the sacred rites of the bull-grappling first took place. The World Tree is represented in Minoan-Mycenaean iconology between two sacrificial animals as a symbol of the vegetative cycle that parallels the seasonal sacrifices and the sacrifices of the animal's blood poured beneath the tree to fertilize it. Pillars in the Pillar Crypts at the Knossos temple-complex are made of ancient olive trees from the sacred grove. Likewise, columns, pillars, and trees on signet rings and gems are depicted between sacrificial animals to illustrate this same concept. The most remarkable depiction of this iconography is found at the Lion Gate at Mycenae where two lions flank a column with celestial discs at the column's top.

The animals in the iconography seem to be both sacrifices and guardians to the World Tree, Sacred Pillar or column. Although instances are somewhat common where celestial spheres or discs are part of the iconography, it should be noted that the archetype of the World Tree in many mythologies is often a symbol of the axis of the earth connecting its poles or connecting the sphere of the earth with the spheres of the heavens and the underworld. The sacrifice of the bulls in Minoan-Mycenaean ideology is linked to the continuing rejuvenation not only of the celestial bodies but to the forces of the earth in connection with the forces of the heavens and the underworld. Evans describes painted reliefs from the porticoes above the Northern Entrance Passage at the northeast section of the temple-complex where sacred olive trees make up the background for the bull-grappling events (III: 176). In these magnificent and enormous depictions of the bull, the sacred act of the sacrifice of the animal is linked to the World Tree and performed at its base. Moreover, the figures in these bull-grappling scenes on the frescoes are women, most likely the priestesses of the temple-complex.

Evans comments that the sacred olive grove was more than just a place to sacrifice the bull. It was the scene of events orchestrated by the priestesses in conjunction with the bulls that were about to be sacrificed. Evans states that the High Priestess herself as representative of the Goddess is seen in the Miniature Fresco at Knossos: "her Pillar shrine is set in the middle of the Grand Stands occupied by the crowds of spectators—like the Royal Box at a Court Theatre" (III: 207). Evans' thorough study of bull-grappling is based on depictions from the painted reliefs and frescoes at the Northern Entrance Passage at Knossos, from the gold cups from the Vapheio Tomb, and from the gypsum slabs from the vestibule of the "Atreus" Treasury at Mycenae as well as from seal, lentoid, and gem stone carvings (III: 177–202). Two types of events displayed on these artifacts clearly indicate that the priestesses are arousing and capturing the bull before its sacrifice; each of these events finds parallels in later Greek mythology. The first event is to net the bull, and the second event is to use a cow decoy to arouse the bull.

In the first event, the bulls are driven along the bottom of a wooded glen with rocky steeps on either side; this is most likely a glen similar to the glen of the sacred olive grove on the northeast corner of the Knossos temple-complex. Evans states: "The animals were thus hurried forward on a kind of obstacle race towards the point where their wild career was checked by a rope cradle stretched across the course between two olive-trees, to the trunks of which the ropes were made fast" (III: 181). The bull that was caught in the net was most likely the bull chosen for sacrifice. On a gold cup from the Vapheio Tomb, the shape of the net holding one bull is that of a crescent moon connecting the bull with the moon in the observer's eye. By checking the headlong rush of the animals, the animals not caught in the net could be ambushed and grappled with. In one depiction, a priestess springs forward to lock both legs and arms around the bull's horns "in such a way that it is not in his power to transfix her" (III: 182). With her full weight thrown on the bull's head, she is able to twist his head as if to break his neck.

The name of the moon goddess Dictynna appears on the Mycenaean Linear B Tablets and is translated in Greek as *diktyon* or "net." In Greek mythology, Dictynna is pursued by Minos, the Cretan King, for nine months because of his lust for her. She is said to have jumped into the sea to escape Minos and is rescued by the fisherman's nets, hence the fisherman use her name to describe their fishing nets; the *diktyon* also refers to a hunter's net. The Greek myth might be a reversal of the chase of Minos and Dictynna where instead of the priestess or goddess chasing the bull, an animal associated in Greek mythology with the Cretan King Minos, Minos is depicted chasing the goddess. Fortunately, this patriarchal interpretation leaves the name of Dictynna and her association with the net, the moon, and the gestation cycle intact. Dictynna, Britomartis, and Eileithyia are aspects of the Mother Goddess of Minoan-Mycenaean mythology that represent the net as birth-giving source of life. In the bull-grappling event of the Minoan-Mycenaean culture, the net may be seen as a symbol of the birth of the new cycle. The birth and re-birth or resurrection of the bull may be represented by his capture in the net, his death, and the resurrection of a new life or cycle in the heavens.

In the second type of event, a decoy cow is used to lure the bull. On another gold cup from the Vapheio Tomb, there are three scenes depicting the successive stages or episodes of the event: "In the first scene the bull is depicted nosing the cow's trail; in the second his treacherous companion engages him in amorous converse, of which her raised tail shows the sexual reaction" and in the third scene "the herdsman takes advantage of this dalliance to lasso the mighty beast by his hind leg" (Evans, III: 183–84). The bull willingly follows the decoy cow to the altar checked only by a rope around his hind leg. In all three scenes of the bull-grappling, Evans notes that there is the same olive tree depicted directly behind the bull, thus establishing the fact that all three scenes take place in the sacred olive grove and that all three scenes are of the same bull making the art "a continuous toreutic work" (III: 184). Evan's interpretation of the decoy cow on the Vapheio cup is convincing and, more importantly, it sheds much light on the Greek myth of Minos and Pasiphaë.

The Greek myth of Minos, the Cretan ruler during the late Minoan-Mycenaean period, contains two themes with celestial imagery. The first recurrent imagery in the myth is that of the takeover of Crete and the worship of the Mother Goddess and subsequent devolution of the astronomer priestesses. The importance of the bull in the reigning power among the gods and men is demonstrated by Zeus' abduction of Minos' mother, Europa, whom Zeus seduces in the form of a white bull; Minos is one of Europa's three children with Zeus. Minos, therefore, is a sacred king, perhaps the symbolic name of a new lineage of Cretan Mycenaean kings establishing their right to reign in Crete, and he is descended from the father god as the sacred bull. After having fathered Minos and his two brothers, Zeus leaves Europa, and she marries Asterius. Asterius, Europa's second husband, is associated with the stars, and as ruler, he controls the rituals formally associated with the astronomer priestesses. Through the influence of Zeus, Asterius and Minos, the powers of the bull, the sun, the moon and the stars have been taken over by masculine figures.

The other theme in the myth of Minos is the theme of the dissolution of the Sacred Marriage rituals of the astronomy priestesses. When Minos claims his right to reign, Poseidon sends him a sacred white bull and instead of sacrificing it, he chooses one of his own bulls. Poseidon punishes him by creating a lust for the bull in Minos' wife, Pasiphaë. Pasiphaë, a daughter of the sun god Helius and the nymph Crete, confides in Daedalus, the famous architect, to build a hollow wooden bull that she can slip inside with her hind quarters thrust in its legs and her vagina exposed for the bull to mount. Her subsequent mating with the sacred bull produces the Minotaur, a monster with the body of a man and the head of a bull (Graves, I: 293). In this myth the Sacred Marriage of the goddess and the bull becomes a woman committing bestiality in order to satisfy her unnatural lust; the punishment for her lust is her monstrous offspring, a bull that lives on to destroy Greek lives in his labyrinth home at Knossos where every nine years he devours Athenian youths. Again, the Sacred Marriage and the powers of the celestial deities, represented by Pasiphaë as daughter of the sun, and the Minotaur as descended from the sacred bull, are diminished by their horrendous associations.

Both bull-grappling events are centered on the amorous relationships between the goddess and the bull. In the first event, the bull is led into the net of Dictynna, the life-giving aspect of the goddess. Like the love chase that ensues in Greek mythology, the goddess as the net and the god as the bull come together in a sacred union that symbolizes the birth and re-birth of a new cycle of life on the earth and in the heavens. In the bull-grappling event with the decoy cow, emphasis is also placed on the union of the goddess and the bull. Both events are part of the sacrifice; the union of the two powers, whether a love chase or a sacred union, capture the most intense moments of life, as the sacrifice will capture the most intense moments of death. The bull is therefore led to the sacrificial altar as part of the *hieros gamos*. This life-in-death theme in Minoan-Mycenaean culture illustrates the vibrant love for life of a culture that embraces both life and death in one instance. Life-in-death reassures the culture that a new cycle will follow the old as inevitably as the heavenly bodies renew their cycles in what Mircea Eliade calls "the eternal return" (12). The dance of life, like the dance of the goddess in the labyrinth of the sacred grove, is a dance of death.

The bull-grappling event that most closely resembles the Sacred Marriage or *hieros gamos* is the cow decoy event. It is not far fetched to speculate that this event spurred on the imagination of the Greek story-tellers to invent the tale of Pasiphaë and the bull to disclaim the power of the goddess and the bull. Pasiphaë, unlike Dictynna, Britomartis, and Aphaia does not escape punishment for her union with the divine bull in Greek mythology. Her punishment furthers the suffering of the Greeks by the Minoans in the form of a monster that preys on the Athenian youth. Each nine years when the Athenian youths are sent to dance with the bull in the labyrinth, the dance of the Sacred Marriage in the sacred grove of olive trees at the northeast corner of the Knossos temple-complex becomes a death dance for the Athenians. In the Sacred Marriage of Ariadne to Theseus, the hero who comes to save the Athenian youths, Ariadne, as daughter of Minos and Pasiphaë, is symbolically deserted much as the labyrinth dance at Crete was abandoned in the Greek assimilation of the Minoan culture (Graves, I: 303). When left on the island of Naxos, Aridane is rescued by Dionysus, the bull god, to live forever in the sky as Corona Borealis, somewhat re-establishing the goddess to her former stature, or at least retaining her as a memory rather than a part of a living ritual.

The Minoan-Mycenaean ritual of the sacrifice of the bull takes place, according to Evans, in the Pillar Crypt of the temple. At Ayia Triada there is a Pillar Crypt for sacrifice, and there are two Pillar Crypts at the Knossos temple-complex: one Pillar Crypt at Knossos is in the Priestesses' Villa at the northeast section of the complex, and the other Pillar Crypt at Knossos is in the center of the main building of the complex whose doors open to the Central Court. It might be suggested that the reason for the two locations might be due to the fact that the Priestesses' Villa is an older structure and nearer to the original sacred olive grove where the bull-grappling events took place. The location of the sacrifice in the Pillar Crypt near the Central Court seems to be more of a central location able to accommodate the large crowds that the Minoan complex once entertained at its peak. This Pillar Crypt is also near to the Temple Repositories where the *xoana* of the Mother Goddess are housed and most likely displayed at rituals and ceremonies; it houses the immense statue of the Mother Goddess as well. The Throne Room of the High Priestess with her lustral basin for ritual re-birth and the large stone bucrania are within close proximity, and a Tripartite Shrine, much like the tripartite seat the High Priestess uses to watch the bull-grappling events, adorns the outside of these chambers. The bull easily would be led up to this location on the ramp passage of the northeast corridor that is decorated with the Fresco of the Bull, which depicts the sacred olive trees as a background reminiscent of the original sacred trees.

For the bull sacrifice at the Priestesses' Villa, the bull would be led in a similar manner through the actual olive grove to the Megaron of the Villa. In the pillar hall of the Megaron, "a triple division, a raised *tribunal*, with its *cancelli* and *exedra*," in the central niche is the seat of honor for the High Priestess (Evans, II: 406). Evans compares this seat to the later seats of honor of the Archon Basileus of the High Priests in the Greek Megaron and to the later Christian church seats in the Early Christian Basilica. A doorway in the northwest corner of the inner section of the Megaron gives access to the Pillar Crypt which is, according to Evans, of "a finer construction than any other known example of such cult chambers." The Pillar in the crypt, made from the original sacred olive tree, is set on square gypsum pavement which is bordered by a "sunken channel" that is oriented east-west of the pillar: "The vats in this case, taken in connection with the sunken square and shallow channel, were clearly part of a system designed for draining off and collecting the liquid offering poured before the sacred pillar" (406).

It is here where the bull is sacrificed and his blood poured into the channel at the base of the Sacred Pillar or World Tree to return the offering to the earth ensuring the re-birth of a new cycle of life. First, the bull is struck on his forehead with the Sacred Axe, and then a dagger is stuck in his neck to allow the blood to flow into the bull's head rhytons or sacral vessels (Burkert 36). The blood is poured in an east-west direction, the directions which symbolize life and death: "To conclude the Eleusinian Mysteries two vessels of a special form were filled—with water?—and then overturned, one towards the west and one towards the east, while to the heavens one cried 'rain!' and to the earth 'conceive!'—in Greek a play on words: *hye—kye*" (Burkert 73). It seems that the bull sacrifice has the same ideological base as the Eleusinian Mysteries, or the sacrifice to the Grain Mother. Both call to their deities to let the water or blood of life resurrect the energies of the earth and the heavens.

The bull is sacrificed at the base of the World Tree by the priestesses using the implement of The Double Axe. Nilsson comments that The Double Axe is never seen in the hands of a male figure and is always carried by women (226). These women, the priestesses of the temple-complex, were responsible for the bull sacrifice most likely using axes made of bronze. What began as a tool used for sacrifice, which was often heavy and unornamented, evolved into a symbol of the bull sacrifice. The sacrificial axes that were discovered in a deposit at the temple-complex at Knossos dating to the late Chalcolithic Era, were obviously used for utilitarian purposes (Evans, I: 198). On the gems and seal impressions from the Minoan-Mycenaean culture, the axe is often depicted above the Bucrania; the axe is also depicted above the Sacred Pillar or Sacred Tree on seal inscriptions or Linear B Tablets (Evans, IV: 344). It obviously evolved from a sacrificial tool to a sacred implement represented in abundance.

Ornamental axes, discovered by the hundreds in the temples of the Minoan-Mycenaean culture, were otherwise used to determine the standstills of the moon in The Horns of Taurus at the Winter Solstice using the Pleiades and Aldebaran as siting markers. When placed in a hole at the center of the bucrania, the two sides of the axe, whose shape represents the waxing crescent of the moon and the waning crescent of the moon, measure the nineteen moons in the lunar cycle. On the crescents, which are back to back to form the shape of the axe, holes or circles mark each moon in the cycle. If the moon count of The Double Axe begins at the lowest tip of the right crescent or what would be the center of the "U" of The Horns of Consecration, the ninth moon would be at the top of the right crescent. To jump The Horns of the Bull would be to move from the ninth year to the tenth; nine and a half years is exactly half of the nineteen year cycle. Perhaps this is the reason that the Minos of Greek mythology requires the Athenian youths to come to Crete as a sacrifice in the ritual of jumping of the bull's horns every nine years. A particularly ornate ritual Double Axe from the Palace at Zakros, represents three full nineteen year cycles of the moon with each circle marking an annual moon. Not all The Double Axes have holes or circles to mark the moon; however, those that are particularly ornate have moon markings. Perhaps these axes belonged to the astronomer priestesses.

The fact that two bulls were often sacrificed lends meaning to the title of The Double Axe as well as to the sets of two bucrania found at the Minoan-Mycenaean temples. A syllabic sign in the Linear B script that is used as an abbreviation of the Greek word *zeugos* or "couple" accompanies the records of the temples where two bulls are sacrificed: "This syllabogram is ZE and can be used to designate a pair of horses or a pair of wheels, but in a certain number of cases, coupled with the ideogram of the bull it means 'a pair of bulls'" (Godart 73). On tablets at the Knossos temple-complex, there are numerous records of two bulls being sacrificed at one time. Two bulls, never more than two, are recorded in these documents. The bulls are described by their colors, such as black or mottled, and they are often delineated as to their weight and size, but they are always in pairs. Tablets from Knossos and Pylos obviously document bulls that were to be used in a ritual sacrifice (Godart 74–6). The syllabogram ZE might have been used as the first two letters of the name of the Greek god "Zeus" as an indication that Zeus be associated with the bull.

The Ayia Triada Sarcophagus has the most detailed portrayal of a Minoan-Mycenaean sacrifice where two bull calves are being led to the altar in a procession on one side of the sarcophagus, and a bull is being sacrificed on the other side of the sarcophagus. At the head of the procession, one man carries a bucrania while two men follow him carrying the bull calves. Three priestesses prepare the altar for sacrifice; one is playing a lyre and the other carries two libation vessels that will most likely hold the blood of the sacrificed calves. A third priestess seems to be pouring a liquid into a vessel at the base of two very ornate Double Axes atop two columns. On the other side of the sarcophagus, a bull is tied to a sacrificial table with its blood pouring into a vessel below the table. Three priestesses approach the altar in a procession accompanied by a man who plays a flute. A fourth priestess prepares the altar, which is decorated with two sets of bucranium, The Double Axe on a column, and lunar and solar discs (Logiadou-Platonos 26–7). In these depictions, The Double Axe, the column of the Sacred Tree, The Horns of Consecration, the sacrifice of the bull, and the role of the astronomer priestesses reveal the flourish of a ceremony which celebrates death and re-birth.

The sacrifice of the bull, the Sacred Marriage of The Goddess and the Bull, and the ritual dedications to the bull throughout the Minoan-Mycenaean culture reflect the culture's belief in the combined powers of The Goddess and Bull to regenerate the energies of life by measuring and celebrating the cycles of heaven and earth. The dedication to the relationship of these two deities allows for a spectrum of goddess worship with attention paid to the masculine forces. To establish the bull as the deity named by the Mycenaean culture as "Zeus" is a more difficult task than delineating and describing the aspects of the Mother Goddess. With the scant amount of information as to the naming of the bull deity, it is safe to assume that a name indeed did exist, but it would be safer to assume personification of the bull or the naming of the bull was a minor part of the Mycenaean belief system compared to the representation of the bull in its animal form. The bull in animal form as a force of masculine energy is fully represented in the bucrania, The Horns of Consecration, the bull rhytons, the Sacred Marriage and The Double Axe.

However, the name of "Zeus" does appear on clay tablets from Knossos that list dedications to the deities, as well as from those tablets from Pylos and Knossos that indicate the syllabogram *ZE* for the sacrifice of two bulls. The name "Zeus" appears on clay tablets from Knossos where oil deliveries are made in "'the month Deukios, to Zeus (?) Diktaios'" (Burkert 43). At Pylos, a long list of gifts details the dispatch of gold vessels and men or women, presumably as slaves, to a series of deities one of which states "'to the Zeus sanctuary,' 'for Zeus, Hera, Drimios the son of Zeus', here delegating one man for Zeus and one woman for Hera" (Burkert 43).

In Pylos, which is on the mainland with stronger Mycenaean influences than Knossos, the tablets list a "Zeus Priest" or *diwijeu* associated with the goddess *Diwija* (Burkert 45). Although the name appears in the tablets, and the Zeus of Greek mythology was said to have been born in Crete and raised by the nurses of Crete, the Kouretes, his iconography in human form is limited to a very few images of the small figure of a young man coming to the goddess in the hieros gamos or to one particular signet ring where the goddess extends her hand to a young man, her consort or son. Most likely, the full personification of this deity associated with the goddess evolved as son, consort, and finally father in the Iron Age with the assimilation of the Indo-European tribes on the mainland of Greece.

The most spectacular representation of the goddess and the bull is an abstract interpretation of their relationship in the form of celestial discs on what Sir

Arthur Evans calls the "Royal Draught Board." The Royal Draught Board was discovered in the northeast Hall that borders the Central Court at the temple-complex at Knossos; a second board was discovered in the Throne Room at Knossos, and a third was discovered at Mycenae. The boards are made of crystal, gold, ivory and silver inlays on a rectangular background of deep blue or *kyanos* backing. On the Royal Draught Board, these faïence inlays take the form of eighteen discs in the center, directly above a brilliant, blue "U" form. In the center of the "U" are nine bold lines of blue that lead up to eight discs which hover above the "U"; the other discs are inside the "U." Four ivory pieces shaped like the naval stone at Delphi with stellar rays or solar symbols on the bottom were also discovered; these were game pieces for the board (III: 471–81). According to Evans: "In its original condition, with its ivory bands and reliefs still plated with gold, and its crystal plaques and bosses intensifying the glint and glow of silver-foil and cerulean paste beneath them, the Gaming Board itself must have been of truly royal magnificence" (III:480).

The Royal Draught Board is an abstract representation of the relationship of The Goddess and the Bull where the nineteen year cycle is depicted in the brilliance of the night sky. The shimmering discs amidst midnight blues are reminiscent of the night sky where the orb of the moon plays its role against a starlit night. To win the game, the player must travel through eighteen discs to complete the nineteen year cycle of the moon and the sun, using the solar pieces to move through the lunar cycle. The "U" configuration holds the first ten discs with a ladder of nine bold, blue lines in the center, a ladder, perhaps, to climb to the second half of the cycle or to jump The Horns of Consecration. At the top of the board, the other discs are symbolic of the last years of the cycle where the moon and the sun are close together culminating the energies of the celestial bodies. Without the iconography of The Goddess and the Bull, the game board clearly represents their relationship as a celestial event of brilliance. The fact that the Minoan-Mycenaean culture would chose to depict The Goddess and the Bull as a celestial game enhances our appreciation of a culture that both admires and senses the deities as essential to their existence and as part of their gaming at the festival of life. Ready for a new cycle of time, ready for the energies of The Goddess and the Bull to inspire them, and ready to play the game of life, the Minoan-Mycenaeans reach out to us to renew our existence through their art and culture.

Chapter Four

Time-Keepers

With the advent of the Iron Age, the archetype of The Goddess and the Bull transforms significantly in the Mediterranean cultures as well as in Europe. The dominant characteristic of the Iron Age cultures is, of course, the discovery of the use of iron and other metals; however, in terms of modern warfare, the most outstanding change in this era is the subsequent use of iron for weaponry, especially in the creation of the iron sword. Two major mythological wars, the Trojan War in the Mediterranean and the Táin Bó Cuailnge in Ireland, base their cycle of warfare and kingship on the nineteen year cycle of the moon and the sun. The role of the Goddess diminishes in the face of warfare and the evolving patriarchy; however, she is still a presence of feminine strength and support for the bull, her resource. As goddess, queen, or woman, the ideology of the Goddess remains a part of the mythology. The poets still chant her presence and the priestesses still practice her rituals. In Greek mythology, she is present in the myths and rituals of Dionysus, son of Zeus, and in the Celtic mythology of the British Isles, she is Queen Maeve of the Táin Bó Cuailnge. By the end of the Iron Age, the Goddess is still present in Celtic poetry of Amergin and Taliesin as the Goddess of the Cauldron of Life, the regenerator par excellence with her son, the Bard.

The Iron Age, despite the evolution of the archetype of The Goddess and the Bull, does present a contribution in technology that former Neolithic and Bronze Age cultures do not. It is in the Iron Age that the most advanced technology occurs in the recording of the cycles of the moon, the stars, and the sun. In fact, although our present culture is far more advanced than the Iron Age in technological achievement, it has not applied the sophisticated technology of the Iron Age for the use of the people in terms of calendar cycles. We measure the cycles on the computer, but we do not live by these cycles or have any common knowledge of them. In a sense, the technology we gained from the Iron Age in terms of celestial awareness has been lost to the common knowledge of the culture. The two outstanding calendar devices the Iron Age has revealed to us, the Antikythera Device of the Mediterranean peoples and the Coligny Calendar of the Europeans, have yet to be recognized and used by the people as they once were. Perhaps a study of the development of these devices will lead our culture to the re-discovery of the cycles of time to create archetypes suitable to demonstrate the emphasis and knowledge of the heavens vital to our understanding of the cycles of life.

The evolution of The Goddess and the Bull in the Iron Age is most easily traced to the Greek rituals and myths that follow the Minoan-Mycenaean culture. In Classical Greece, the oldest recorded sacrificial animal is the bull that the priestesses of Hera at Argos dedicated to the deities (Burkert 96). In the sacrifice of the bull the sacred axe of the Minoans and the sacred knife used for the sacrifice are carried by a priestess in a basket on her head in the procession of the sacrifice of the bull. The bull is sacrificed in the name of Zeus or Dionysus and the all the priestesses present must illicit the sacrificial cry, marking the emotional climax where "life screams over death" (Burket 56). Although the sacrifice of the bull is to the male deities descended from the Cretan Zeus, the priestesses are still a vital part of the transformative process. The blood is collected in a basin and sprayed over the altar and against the sides to stain the altar with blood in much the same manner that the Minoans poured the blood at the base of the sacred tree or pillar in the Pillar Crypts. The death of the bull, like the sacrifices of the Minoan-Mycenaean culture, represents the reconstitution of the life of the animal where one life cycle continues from death to re-birth. The sacrifice is timely, potent, and requires the participation of the women of the culture.

Although the bull was sacrificed to many deities in the Classical Pantheon, the Attic calendar festivals reveal the most telling facts as to the role of The Goddess and the Bull in Greek culture. In the Greek lunar calendar of Attica, the most important bull sacrifice takes place on the full moon of the Summer Solstice or on the full moon of the month of *Skiraphorion*; it is called the *Dipolieia* or the *Bouphonia*. On a calendar-frieze from Attica, a young man with boots and a cloth about his waist, dressed similar to "The Prince with the Lilies" on the Minoan fresco at Knossos, holds a Double Axe above the victim of the *Bouphonia*, a bull. (Simon Plate 2). The altar for the sacrifice was on the northeast corner of the Acropolis where a bronze table, the same color of yellow as the Double Axe, was used for the sacrifice; the table is believed to be "a relic of the Mycenaean Age." After the sacrifice, the bull's hide was "stuffed to restore the animal to the appearance of life" (Simon 8–9). The use of the Double Axe, the Minoan costume of the sacrificer, and the location of the sacrifice at the northeast corner of the temple using a bronze table all indicate the influence and purposeful retention of Minoan-Mycenaean culture. Even the idea that the bull will begin a new life after death is retained.

According to Erika Simon in her book *Festivals of Attica*: "In spite of all development in Greek thought and art, religious rites tended to be preserved pure and unchanged." (11) This may be true concerning the astronomer priestesses of the Minoan-Mycenaean culture who performed the bull-grappling events; even though the priestesses who wear the basket on their heads and give the sacrificial cry are not depicted on the Attic calendar frieze, they would have been present according to Simon. Additionally, the core of the ideology of the regeneration and re-birth of the bull is obviously present in this instance. On an *Oinochoe* or wine jug depicting the *Dipolieia*, two bulls with one black bull on top of the altar and the other white bull below the altar are depicted (Simon Plate 6). This may represent the death of the sacrificed bull as the black bull on the altar and his ghost or re-incarnated other under the altar. It may represent the two bulls being sacrificed or more than likely, it also may suggest the two phases of the moon, in its dark and full phase as the life and death of the lunar cycle, thus establishing the celestial connections of the sacrifice to the heavens.

Like the *Dipolieia*, the festivals of the rites of Dionysus on the Attica lunar calendar have Iron Age representatives of the both The Goddess and the Bull. Here, the Goddess is represented as the nurses of Dionysus in the *Lenaia* festival, as the *basilinna* or queen and wife of Dionysus in the *Anthesteria* or festival of the *hieros gamos*, and as Maenads or *Gerairai* in the sacrifice and resurrection of the god in the *City Dionysia* festival. The first festival, the *Lenaia*, is celebrated on the seventh full moon of the Attica calendar where the nurses are represented in the star cluster of Coma Berenices in the night sky. It is the first celebration at the end of winter that marks the coming of the vegetation spirit of the spring or The Dying God known as Dionysus, the son of Zeus by Semele, the earth-mother goddess. The *Anthesteria* or sacred marriage is celebrated around the next full moon where the constellations of Corona Borealis and Boötes represent the wife of Dionysus and Dionysus, respectively. Dionysus, in his bull form or as a phallus, is sacrificed and resurrected in the *City Dionysia* around the full moon of the next month. The festivals, known as the Dionysian Mysteries, are just long enough to represent three full cycles of the nineteen year cycle of the moon and the sun, a lifetime to the ancients.

In the *Lenaia* which takes place in the month of *Gamelion*, the nurses of Dionysus are representatives of the birthing and nursing aspect of the Mother Goddess for her consort and son. They are derived from the Minoan-Mycenaean birthing aspect of the Mother Goddess. In a hymn of invocation engraved on a stone in Palaikastro, Crete, the nurses or foster-mothers are referred to as "the shielded Nurturers" (Gimbutas, *Living Goddesses* 235). The Greeks call them the Kouretes of the Dictaean Zeus who leap and dance with cymbals and drums to welcome the god back to life from the Underworld opening in his cave sanctuary. Their names are Eileithyia, Britomartis and Dictynna, and their symbol is the amniotic water of life. In the Greek festival, they are a procession of priestesses who dance and sing for the god to appear to the people from the sacred waters of Lerna. In the *Bakkhai*, Euripides says the god is welcomed by the women and "from the earth comes flowing milk, flowing/ Wine, flowing nectar of bees!" (174–75). The priestesses birth the god and nurse Dionysus, the god of wine, with the water and milk of life. Literally, they mix or *louch* the wine to make it milky when adding water to it. This brings the spirits of the wine or the herbs in the wine, which are wormwood, anise, and fennel, to an active state making the substance psychotropic.

In the Lesser Mysteries of Eleusis performed before the *Anthesteria*, which is the full moon of the month of *Anthesterion*, water as an inspirational element for the initiates is used without the wine (Mylonas 242). In the festival of the Lesser Mysteries, the initiate must be cleansed in the river with her or his sacrifice of a sow to Persephone, the goddess of the spring, before she or he receives the rites. The initiate is then brought to the temple and a liknon or winnowing fan is placed above her or his head. She or he is then received by the goddess of the grain, Demeter, in her or his preparation for her or his initiation into the Greater Mysteries in the fall. The purpose of this ancient ritual is to prepare the initiate for the rituals in much the same manner that the wine and water of The Dying God is prepared by the priestesses in the Dionysian Mysteries. Both celebrations take place in Athens and the nearby town of Eleusis where Greeks are initiated into the Mysteries through the water and wine of life.

The representative in the night sky of the priestesses who prepare water and wine for the initiates is the star cluster of Coma Berenices. Coma Berenices is a star cluster that is associated with the goddess. It was named in the third century BC after Ptolemy II's wife, Queen Berenice who sacrificed her hair to the goddess if her husband would return safely from battle, the world of death and dying. Patterned after the myth of the goddess Isis, who sacrifices her hair in order that her husband, Osiris, return from the dead, Berenice is aptly deified in ancient Egypt. The theme of bringing back the male deity from the realm of the dead finds its metaphor in the Dionysian Mysteries where Dionysus is called from the waters of Lerna by the priestesses. Additionally, the star cluster is said by Vergil to represent a "new" conception that the Greeks had of the ascendance of the souls of the dead. According to Vergil, the Hellenistic Age popularized the idea that if souls were purified by the Lesser Mysteries, they would be as chaff tossed into the liknon to ascend to aerial space for eternity (Nilsson, *Dionysiac* 370). The chaff is represented by the cloudy debris of Coma Berenices where the souls are believed to ascend. The star cluster, therefore, is both a metaphor for regeneration and the eternal renewal of life in the heavens. Like the star cluster of the Pleiades that marks the coming of winter on the calendars of the ancients, the star cluster of Coma Berenices marks the initiation rites and the calling of the god back from the dead of winter to spring through the cleansing water and inspirational wine of the Mysteries.

After the initiates are prepared for the Mysteries, the *Anthesteria* is celebrated in the full moon of the month of *Anthesterion* where the *hieros gamos* or sacred marriage takes place. Here, the role of the goddess is represented by the *basilinna*, which literally means the "queen" or the wife of Dionysus. The role of the wife or consort of the deity is easily identified with the aspect of the Mother Goddess as consort to the bull in Minoan-Mycenaean culture. Although the Minoan labyrinth dance of the bride or the bull-grappling event of the decoy cow is not present in the Greek ritual of the sacred marriage, the *basilinna* is used to lure Dionysus as the bull into the bull's stall or Boukoleion near the Agora. The event was strictly secret. The wedding procession took place at night where the bride waited for her groom to arrive. According to Simon:

> A fragmentary calyx-krater in Tübingen shows Dionysus' bride sitting on the bed and being served by Eros. Here, Dionysus is followed by a satyr with the typical chorus, but the scene is very serious. Because the bride is identified by an inscription as Ariadne, the picture shows an etiological myth closely connected with the sacred wedding at the Anthesteria.
> (Simon 97)

In Greek mythology, Ariadne was abandoned by Theseus on the island of Naxos and married to Dionysus. Her crown, the constellation of Corona Borealis, which is a tiny circlet of stars to the east of Boötes, represents her in the night sky.

Dionysus is represented in the Dionysian Mysteries and in the comedies and tragedies that were performed at the festival of the ninth full moon called the *City Dionysia*. In Athens, the god appears as a bull and as an erect phallus, both appropriate symbols for rejuvenation, resurrection, and fertility. He is welcomed in a procession through the city streets masked as a bull or presented as a column-shaped or phallic-shaped idol, and then he is brought to the Boukoleion for the hieros gamos. In Euripides *Bakkhai*, Dionysus changes into a bull when Pentheus confines him to the bull's stall in the palace, and he emerges as "bullified" leading the Maenads to the sacrifice (1056). The sacrifice in this play is Pentheus as a bull or "bull-calf" and not the god himself, still the Chorus urges for Pentheus to be let free of his "net" to be sacrificed at the foot of a tree he uses for refuge (Scene V). The reference of the net that Euripides uses several times in the play and the two bulls, Dionysus and Pentheus, recalls the net and two sacrificed bulls of Minoan-Mycenaean culture. Moreover, the use of the bull and the column or phallic-shaped idol is reminiscent of the Minoan-Mycenaean bull sacrifice where the sacrifice is performed at the base of the sacred olive tree or World Tree, a symbol similar to a column. In the final scene of the play, Dionysus appears as the god, masked and potent much like his image in the *City Dionysia* procession.

The Greek festival of the *City Dionysia* and Euripides' play both contain an element of extreme violence in the bull sacrifice and *sparagmos,* or the ripping and eating of raw flesh; neither is depicted in the Minoan-Mycenaean culture. *Sparagmos* is performed in the play by the Maenads who are represented in the festival as Dionysus' priestesses, *The Gerairai.* The violence and *sparagmos* of the Dionysian Mysteries is echoed in the myths of Dionysus where shortly after his birth, the god is torn into shreads at Hera's orders, and then he is reconstituted and brought back to life by his grandmother, Rhea. A tree sprouts from the soil where his blood has fallen (Euripides *Bakkhai* 125–65). Immediately, the resurrection of the sacrificed god is emphasized as is his ability to be re-born as the World Tree. However, the violence accompanying his birth and the anger of Hera might represent the antagonism of the priestesses of this ancient Mother Goddess when they are forced to accept a new, powerful male deity into their Bronze Age ideology. In an historical sense, the introduction of the Dionysian Mysteries in the Iron Age reflects the violence imposed on the cults of the Mother Goddess. Dionysus meets with opposition in Thrace, Thebes, Orchomenus and Argos, the site of Hera's strongest cult.

The sacrifice of the bull in the Dionysian myths and rituals is viewed in the night sky in the rising of the constellation of Boötes and in the setting of the constellation of Taurus. This happens in the ninth moon of the month of *Elaphebolion* on the Attic calendar where the stellar and lunar drama is complemented with the solar event of the Vernal Equinox. As Taurus the Bull sinks slowly below the horizon in the west, he is devoured by the sun's rays in a violent death. He is pursued by Mars, the red planet of war and death, as he descends into the waters below the horizon. The Greeks call attention to another celestial body that ties into the myths of Dionysus by naming a spring constellation after Dionysus' son, Boötes. In Greek myth, Boötes is a herdsman who is killed by his fellow shepherds. Like Dionysus, he dies a tragic death. When his body is found by his daughter, Erigone, she hangs herself. Boötes is placed in the night sky as a constellation, and his daughter is placed beside him as the constellation of Virgo (Staal 153–53). The primary star of Boötes, Arcturus, rises in the east as an indication that the sacrifice of The Dying God is happening. Arcturus, a very bright yellow-orange star marks the beginning of *Elaphebolion*. It is complemented by the death of Taurus on the western horizon.

The myths and rituals of The Goddess and the Bull in the Iron Age in the Mediterranean are based on an interest in the cycles of the moon, the sun, and the stars. Although astronomy is a central focus in the myths, according to Robert Graves, the evolution of the myths and their corresponding references to astronomy also follow an historical and political process. Graves asserts that the process starts when the one year service of the Mother Goddess' consort was changed with the Aeolian and Ionian invasions of the Hellenes in the early second millennium BC. The consort, as Zeus or Dionysus, who was replaced each year at the end of winter or early spring, is subsequently replaced every nine and one half years, or at the mid-point of the nineteen year cycle. Graves calls half of the nineteen year cycle "The Great Year Cycle" ("Introduction" 18–19). Counting years in the cycle begins at the bottom of the "U" configuration or bucrania; therefore, mid-way through the ninth year, the count jumps from the right tip of the horns of the "U" configuration or bucrania to the left tip of The Horns of the Bull. In other words, it jumps The Horns of the Bull. This would prove an obvious junction to end the reign of one consort and begin the cycle of another. Graves goes on to state that "a closer approximation of solar and lunar time" was then used to extend the reign of the consort to a nineteen year cycle or "Greater Year."

When the Achaean invasions in the thirteenth century BC "seriously weakened the matrilocal tradition," the reign of the consort was finally recognized as kingship and his reign became his entire lifetime. According to Graves: "It seems that the king now contrived to reign for the term of his natural life; and when the Dorians arrived, towards the close of the second millennium, patrilineal succession became the rule" (19). In mythology, Graves sees this evolution as the Olympian system where "a compromise is reached between the Hellenic and pre-Hellenic peoples; a divine family of six gods and six goddesses, headed by the co-sovereigns Zeus and Hera and a Council of Gods" is formed. Graves asserts: "Patrilineal descent, succession, and inheritance discourage further myth-making; historical legend then begins and fades into the light of common history" (20). In terms of the archetype of The Goddess and the Bull, this proves true. The Dionysian Mysteries celebrate the one year cycle of the Mother Goddess and the bull where life energies are rejuvenated each year in reverence to the celestial bodies of the night sky. The Mysteries are based on ritual, myth and drama that continue the belief in the regenerative powers of the deities. However, The Goddess and the Bull are not part of

the schemata of the emerging literature of the patriarchy that represents the
nine year cycle or "The Great Year Cycle" and the nineteen year cycle or the
"Greater Year" as the reign of kingship and duration of warfare.

In Homer's war saga of the Greek Iron Age, the *Iliad* and the *Odyssey*, the
reign of Priam of Troy was determined to be nineteen years legitimately as
nineteen of his fifty sons were legitimate. However, the Trojan War disrupted
Priam's reign. Instead, the Trojan War and the return of the hero, Odysseus,
involves nineteen years, a symbolic overturn of what might have occurred to
what actually occurs in terms of Greek heroics. The *Iliad* involves the last
months of the final year of the Trojan War, which would be nine and a half
years to the final tenth year, or symbolically "The Great Year Cycle." The war
might symbolize jumping The Horns of the Bull in terms of heroic efforts to
accomplish unthinkable feats and subsequent victories. Odysseus is a major
part of these efforts as a true Iron Age hero; however, he must then go through
a journey, both physical and spiritual, to return home to his wife, Penelope, to
claim his rightful reign as king for the rest of his natural life. Odysseus' journey lasts nine years and in the tenth year, he returns home to Ithaca at night;
Odysseus is asleep and is deposited in the home of a former slave, the swineherd, Eumaeus. In essence, he is reborn when he has completed a "Greater
Year" of adventures, and after he reveals himself to his nurse, Eurycleia, and
to his son, Telemachus, he takes over his kingdom for his lifetime. The Greek
saga establishes the reign of the king in Odysseus' trials in a cycle where he
is re-born to himself and his people as a hero.

In the Iron Age in Europe and the British Isles, the archetype of The Goddess and the Bull undergoes a similar transformation because of the rise of
warfare, the patriarchy and the newly defined reign of a king. The Goddess
and the Bull are represented in the rituals and myths of the people, but they
are rarely found in the literature of the newly established patriarchy. The
major difference between the Iron Age Greek and Celtic cultures is that
women as representatives of the goddess are still found in the war sagas of
the Celtic patriarchy. The role of the goddess, however, has the strongest
representation in ritual in both cultures. The goddess is clearly depicted in
the ritual of the Celtic bull sacrifice or *tarb feis*. Druids, or the educated
class of Celtic culture, consist of both women and men, equally, and as
priestesses and priests, the Druids performed the bull sacrifice in the spring
at the first full moon after the Vernal Equinox, at Beltaine, at the Summer
Solstice, and on other major holidays. The Neolithic stone configurations
and circles were still being used in Iron Age Europe and the British Isles by
the Celtic peoples who celebrated the nineteen year cycle of The Goddess
and the Bull as well as the other cycles of precession marked on the stones.
The Druids enhanced this knowledge by using the stone circles and "U"

configurations to determine their holidays, and they celebrated by sacrificing to the goddesses and gods.

In the *tarb feis*, the maiden or bride aspect of the Mother Goddess is represented by her bird attribute, usually a crane, which symbolizes her role in
the sacred marriage to the bull. Druids wear "a white speckled bird's headdress with fluttering wings" as representatives of the bird aspect of the goddess to perform the sacrifice of two bulls (Ross 83). At the Summer Solstice,
they cut the mistletoe, a sacred vine with hallucinogenic properties, and the
berries fall on to a bull's hide. At Beltaine, two bulls are run between Beltaine
fires or need-fires for purification and then are sacrificed for the Beltaine couple, the May Queen and King, earthly representatives of the sacred marriage.
A spiral or circle dance is performed at the base of the Beltaine Tree, or *bile*.
The goddess' role in the dance is similar to Ariadne's dance of the labyrinth
or "crane dance." Like the Minoan-Mycenaean and Greek bull rituals, the
goddess is represented in the Celtic rituals in the sacred marriage. In all these
rituals the dance takes place, and the presence of the World Tree forms an essential part of the rituals.

The crane-heron, a form adopted exclusively by females in Celtic mythology, is represented on a bronze figurine from the temple of Maiden Castle in
Britain as three women emerging from a bull's back, and it is represented on
a relief from Paris as three cranes on a bull's back (Ross 363). According to
Ross: "Its appearance as a female form of metamorphosis in the insular traditions suggests that it was originally the attribute or shape assumed by some
potent and formidable goddess" (365). Ross states that a complex of images
includes the bull, the cranes on his back, and a willow tree branch felled by
the god, Esus; this complex of images represents the sacred marriage of the
bird and the bull, an ecological phenomenon present in the bird and bull's
symbiotic relationship in the watery marshes of the Celts. According to Ross,
this "bull-tree-wading bird complex" dates from the Urnfield and Hallstatt
cultures onwards (c. 800 BC). Esus, the dying god and the god of war, is depicted as Mars in the Gallo-Roman period, and as both, he is accompanied by
the crane goddesses and the bull and is most likely seen as the sacrificer.
When Aoife, the crane goddess of the early Irish myths dies, and the sacred
crane-bag or *Fir Bolg* holding precious tokens is made from her skin, it is
worn on the neck by the Druids as a symbol of re-birth and rejuvenation, a
major theme in the sacrifice of The Goddess and the Bull. According to Ross,
the role of the crane in this complex is one that eventually becomes associated with protection and war (353).

Women as representatives of the goddess are found in the war sagas of the patriarchy in Celtic mythology. Unlike the Greek Iron Age mythology where the
role of the goddess is one of protection and sovereignty in a strictly passive

sense, the role of goddesses and women in Celtic lore is one of protection and sovereignty in an active sense since women were allowed to participate in warfare. In the great Irish war epic of the *Táin Bó Cuailnge*, Queen Maeve is the protagonist of the war who provokes the central action of the narrative. This warrior queen of Connacht is a vibrant personality who decides to challenge her husband Ailill as to which one of them has brought more power and wealth to the marriage. After displaying their wealth, Maeve decides that she can only be the dominant partner by securing the most powerful bull in Ireland, Donn Cuailnge or The Brown Bull; the Donn Cuailnge must be stolen from the province of Cuailnge, which is defended by the great Celtic hero Cúchulainn, in order that the brown bull may battle her husband's powerful white bull, Finnbennach, The White Bull of Connacht. Finnbennach was born in Maeve's herds, but he has deserted to her husband's herds because he refuses to be ruled by a woman. Bulls represent wealth in this milieu and the bulls in this tale may very well represent the wealth of the patriarchy. The symbolism of Maeve's struggle for dominance over both the white and brown bulls becomes one of challenging the existing patriarchy. Although she does not succeed in overcoming the patriarchy, she does challenge the emerging role of women in it, and she is an obvious representative of the power of The Goddess and the Bull.

Maeve otherwise known as Medb, Meadhbh, Méadhbh, Maev, Meave, or Maive, most likely is a descendent and "apotheosis of several forces and antecedents, including goddesses of territory, fertility, and sovereignty" such as Mór Muman of Munster or the Gaulish Mother Goddess (Mackillop 326). According to Anne Ross in *Celtic Pagan Britain*: "In this type of Celtic ruler-queen then, the mother, mate, and politician, strategist and combatant in war, we may visualize some earthly reflection of the cult concept of the "Mother of the gods.' " (454). Her divine origins are suggested by her strange and magical dominance over males where the sight of her is "sufficient to deprive men of two-thirds of their strength" (Ross 286). Likewise, her associations with the toponymy of Ireland where her urine is said to form the *Fual Medba* or three great dykes large enough for an entire mill to fit in each dyke, attests to her supernatural powers. Maeve's goddess attributes are also demonstrated by her possession of her own sacred tree or *bile* called the *Bile Meidbe*, which parallels the sacred tree or World Tree found in Minoan-Mycenaean culture at the sacrifice of the bull. Finally, she is connected to the bird aspect of the Mother Goddess when associated with the bull, as she is often portrayed with a bird on one of her shoulders (Ross 61).

Like the representatives of the goddess in the Dionysian Mysteries, Maeve possesses both the power to intoxicate and sexually arouse her subjects. Her name is related to the word "mead" which is a Celtic equivalent to the wine of the Dionysian rites. In an age of warfare and warriors, the influence of

Maeve as "Drunk Making Woman" represents her power to inspire the warriors in battle as the Celtic tradition was literally to liberally provide the warriors with alcoholic drinks before battle (Ross 235). Like the mead and wine, Maeve's role as a representative of the goddess is to ensure the continuity of her culture through the ability to inspire the courage to face death and believe in the resurrection of the soul. Her sexuality is also an expression of the importance of the continuity of life over the power of death. Like the bull, Maeve is a representative of fertility and renewal of life. Her sexual desire was so great that she had to be satisfied every day by thirty different men or go one day with the great warrior Fergus *Virogustus,* the choice of men. Celtic custom permits a woman, and especially a queen like Maeve, to take lovers; therefore, Maeve's power for renewal could be increased through her sexuality. As Maeve herself states: " ' daig ni raba-sa riam cen fer ar scath araile ocum' or 'for I have never been without having one man after another with me' " (Ross 300). According to Miriam Robbins Dexter, "Medb enjoyed a long series of husbands, since, again, she was the key to the sovereignty of Ireland, and thus no man could be king unless he was married to her" (107).

Maeve is a divine warrior queen who quests for the power of the regenerative forces through her search for the Donn, or the most potent bull of Ireland. As a figure descendent from the Mother Goddess, her purpose is also to protect her land by securing sovereignty of Ireland and thus retaining the aspect of the Mother Goddess as earth mother. According to Ross, she is "giver of prosperity to the land," "protectress of the flocks and herds," and "more archaic than the gods, she remained tied to the land for which she was responsible and whose most striking natural features seemed to her worshippers to be the manifestation of her power and personality" (297). In this role, her search for the Brown Bull of Cooley, the Donn Cuailnge, begins the Iron Age war saga.

In the story of the Táin Bó Cuailnge, Maeve, her seven sons and their armies chase the Donn Cuailnge to Sliab Cuilinn plundering Northern Ireland and its people as they go. The bull himself is almost captured, but slays fifty heroes and escapes. Cúchulainn, the great hero of Ulster, must face Maeve's forces almost single-handed as his troops have been cursed by the horse goddess, Macha, and are useless in battle. After many successes where Maeve's best warriors have been killed in battle by Cúchulainn, Maeve and her husband, Ailill, are left to battle Cúchulainn with only a small troop of warriors; Cúchulainn has slaughtered nine troops of three thousand men and nothing is left but "a handful of ribs from his chariot out of the frame and a handful of spokes from the wheel." Maeve, however, has succeeded in capturing the Donn Cuailnge and has sent the bull back to her home with his fifty heifers and eight messengers so that the brown bull would be gotten safely away. After her defeat and the loss of her troops, Maeve "got her gush of blood" which fertilizes the land in the immense proportion that represents her goddess stature. When she goes to relieve herself, also in the immense proportions of a goddess, Cúchulainn comes upon Maeve and does not destroy her. He lets her go home saying he is not "a killer of women" (Kinsella 249–50). Maeve's loss of warriors and shedding of her own menstrual blood symbolize the great queen's gift to the land. Her menstrual blood has been shed on the earth to restore life to the land in the same way the blood of the sacrificed bull is poured beneath the sacred tree to restore life to the earth. As an Iron Age representative of the goddess, Maeve has sacrificed part of herself.

Although the battle for power, sovereignty and domination of the land has been fought on the human level in the *Táin*, the battle of supernatural forces takes place when the armies return to Connacht to watch the Donn Cuailnge, Maeve's brown bull, battle Finnbennach, Ailill's white bull. When this battle begins, the Donn plants a hoof on the other bull's horn and holds him there all day until nightfall. Fergus, one of Maeve's warriors, speaks to the Donn, as if the bull has supernatural powers and understands the language of men. He asks the bull to release Finnbennach and fight him in an honorable manner as so many men have died in order for this battle to take place. The Donn releases Finnbennach, and they fight all night on the Ai Plain at Tarba: "That night the bulls circled the whole of Ireland. When the morning came, the men of Ireland saw the Donn Cuailnge coming westward past Cruachan with the mangled remains of Finnbennach hanging from his horns." (Kinsella 252). Wherever the Donn stops, he leaves a part of Finnbennach and the land is named accordingly. When the Donn comes to the border of his own land, mortally wounded, his heart breaks and the battle is over; again, two bulls have been sacrificed in honor of the goddess. The bulls have been sacrificed for the land and have become the land itself in order that it may regenerate from their blood. The cycle of sacrifice and renewal has been fulfilled, and a new cycle may begin for both The Goddess and the Bull.

At the beginning of the *Táin*, there are seven foretales or rémscéla, the last of which is the story of the history and begetting of Donn Cuailnge and Finnbennach. It is here where the magic of the bulls becomes more evident than that which is already demonstrated by the understanding on the part of the Donn to comprehend the language of Fergus in the final battle of the bulls. According to Ross, the magic of the bull to understand human reasoning indicates its divine origin. In the rémscéla of the *Táin*, Ross notes one of many of the bull's magic virtues described by the original storyteller is the bull's ability to hold fifty youths on his back while the youths were engaged in games of "'draughts and assembly and leaping; *another of the magic virtues of the Donn* he would not put them from him nor would he totter under them'"

(214). The mention of both the draught board and the leaping recalls the Minoan-Mycenaean draught board, the bull-leaping activities of their culture, and the relationship of play that the people have with the bull in their worship of The Goddess and the Bull. Ross states that the bull is part of a tradition of "a great supernatural bull, protector of warriors, averter of evil from the province (therefore apotropaic), provider of magical music, of prime importance in Celtic societies, and ensuring the reproductive powers of the herds" (215). The magic of the bulls and their divine origin is evident in their relationship with the people and in their history and begetting.

In the seventh rémscéla, the bulls are begotten when two pig-keepers begin a fight, similar to the fight between Maeve and Ailill, where each claims he has more power and influence than the other. In turn, they represent their owners, the king of the sídh or sacred land of Connacht and the king of the sídh of Munster. Both pig-keepers are "practiced in the pagan arts" as shape-changers (Kinsella 46). As the pig-keepers continue to argue, they change into two birds of prey, two water creatures, two stags, two warriors, two phantoms, two dragons and two maggots. As maggots, one gets into a spring at Cuailnge where a cow drinks it up, and the other gets into a spring in Connacht, the land belonging to Maeve, where a cow drinks it up. From the cows, they are born as the Donn Cuailnge and Finnbennach, respectively. Their eighteen transformations, known as metempsychosis, are symbolic of the nineteen year cycle of the moon and the sun where in their final transformation as the fighting bulls of the *Táin*, they complete the nineteen years through their death. In the rémscéla, the importance of kingship is emphasized as well as the relationships of Maeve as a representative of the goddess with her struggle for power in the patriarchy. Moreover, the concept of metempsychosis and the transmigration of souls is introduced as the basis of the *Táin*. The idea that knowledge is gained and conflict resolved through death, rebirth, and a continuing cycling with the heavenly bodies represented in the nineteen year cycle of the moon and the sun is paramount to the ideology of the Celts as well as other ancient cultures.

The pig-keepers are reminiscent of the pig-keeper Odysseus returns to after his long journey home. As pigs and pig-keepers are associated with death and the journey to the Otherworld or world below, especially in the Eleusinian Mysteries and in Greek mythology, it is only fitting that they become the gate keepers of the transformative process. The bull, in turn, becomes the final transformation because it has the magical powers of understanding and the relationship with the goddess or her representative, Maeve. Thus, the bull is deemed sacrosanct and the representative of the goddess maintains her relationship in the process. In the later roscanna or magical poetry and chants of the Druids, this idea of metempsychosis is emphasized even though the goddess no longer has a dominant role in the mythology. In the roscanna of Amergin, the Irish Bard, and Taliesin, the Welsh Bard, the goddess is the mother of the Bard and the bull is one of the stages of his transformation. Although the roles of the goddess and the bull seem to have diminished, metempsychosis is still represented as the nineteen year cycle of the moon and the sun. The transformative process is reflected in nineteen stages of shape-changing by the poet in order for him to achieve the knowledge of the cycles of life, death and rebirth, and it is reflected in the form of many of the verses that use nineteen lines to express each of these transformations.

In the rosc of Amergin entitled "Duan Amhairghine" or "Amergin's Challenge," Amergin, the first Bard of the Milesians to literally set foot on the shores of Ireland, professes his knowledge in a nineteen line rosc that outlines his stages of transformation. It begins with his profession that he has been the wind across the sea, a flood across the plain, and so on until he reaches the ninth transformation where he makes a leap to become "the salmon of wisdom." Like the leap of the ninth year to the tenth year in Minoan-Mycenaean culture where the moon leaps The Horns of the Bull in its journey half way through the nineteen year cycle, this leap is symbolic of the knowledge attained by the bull jumper, or in this case, the Bard. In both Irish and Welsh mythology, when Fionn mac Cumhaill and Taliesin taste the salmon, they attain the knowledge of life, death and rebirth. Likewise, the Irish hero Cúchulainn develops his salmon leap as a true warrior who gains the knowledge of the poets and priests. It is only fitting that at the moment when the poet jumps The Horns of the Bull, he too attains knowledge. In his continuing transformations, Amergin is "the dark secret of the dolmen" and the shield and spear of battle (Ó Tuathail 10). Here, he attains the knowledge of the stones, which contain the knowledge of the time-keepers of the moon, the sun, and the stars, and he attains the knowledge of the weapons so important to the Iron Age warrior.

Amergin's final transformation is one into the realms of death where he professes that:

> I am the grave of every vain hope
> Who knows the path of the sun, the periods of the moon
> Who gathers the divisions, enthralls the sea,
> Sets in order the mountains, the rivers, the peoples

(Ó Tuathail 10)

His final knowledge comes through death where he is able to be a time-keeper of the moon, the sun and the stars in order to bring these "divisions" of the heavens to the people as inhabitants of the earth. In a sense, by uniting the three sacred realms of the heavens, the earth and the underworld, he becomes a true Druid and priest of the people. With his knowledge of time and the stones, which mark the cycles of the celestial bodies, he has attained true knowledge of the infinite. His metempsychosis is complete through his nineteen transformations through one cycle of the moon and the sun. According to Anthony Murphy in *Island of the Setting Sun: In Search of Ireland's Ancient Astronomers*, "Amergin's claim to tell the ages of the moon is suggestive of the knowledge of lunar cycles, such as the 19-year cycle of the moon" (32).

In the roscanna of the Welsh Bard, Taliesin, The Goddess and the Bull are both part of the transformative cycles of the Bard. In the *Hanes Taliesin*, Taliesin steals his powers from the goddess Ceridwen, who owns the Cauldron of Inspiration and Wisdom. When Ceridwen realizes that Taliesin has stolen the knowledge from her, Taliesin must shape-change into a hare, a fish, a bird, and a grain of wheat while she shape-changes into various forms with him in the chase. After nine transformations, she swallows him and he is reborn as a child from a bag made from the skin of a sacred bird, the crane. Like the Greek and Minoan-Mycenaean culture where the crane is the sacred bird of the Mother Goddess, the crane acts as a protector of Taliesin's spirit, and when he emerges from the crane-bag as a child again, he is loved by Ceridwen as her own child. The Goddess of the Cauldron, a theme which recurs in Welsh mythology, is symbolic of the poet's power and knowledge necessitating from the protection of a feminine deity, albeit she is often represented as a hag or cailleach. Likewise, his transformation from one life to another in the sacred bag of the crane, a goddess associated with the bull in Celtic iconography, is also necessary, like the crane dance of the Minoan-Mycenaean culture, to inspire his growth and contribute to his knowledge.

Taliesin's "Song of Origins" is a rosc that relates his transformative process in all its nineteen stages, one of which is the bull, as opposed to the *Hanes Taliesin* which is a prose piece outlining half of his shape-changing (Matthews 14–18; 281). In the *Cad Goddeu* or "Battle of the Trees," Taliesin's spiritual journey is also in poetic form where the full exposition of his nineteen stages is outlined in its entirety. Here, again, Taliesin professes that in "nine years of enchantment" after being born from the water and the crane bag, he is able to command the power of the trees, the earth, and the stars. Taliesin states: "By the wisest of druids was I made before the world began,/ And I know the star-knowledge from the beginning of Time." (Matthews 299). With the knowledge of "splendid starlight" Taliesin is able to become the Chief Bard of Wales. In "The Hostile Confederacy," Taliesin comes to his full manhood and power when by "the end of his song,/ he will know the starry wisdom." He has been born from the Cauldron of the Goddess and as a bull, goat, and many other forms, he has achieved the title of "wiseman of primal knowledge." (Matthews 312–14). His knowledge of the stars is emphasized in the poetry, and his stage as the bull is mentioned as an essential part of the thematics of the verse. However, it is in the form of the verse that the nineteen years of the cycle of the moon and sun is actualized. Although each form has lost its symbolic meaning to the modern reader, they represent an important transformative process of the heavenly bodies.

The knowledge of the celestial bodies and the tracing of the nineteen year cycle of the moon and the sun became a vital element of the knowledge of the Druids in the Iron Age because of the stone circles and ancient megalithic ruins that formed an essential part of their landscape. By the end of the Bronze Age in Britain, several standing stone sites and stone circles clearly represented the nineteen year cycle of the moon and the sun. The inner "U" constructed at Stonehenge, called "The Bluestone Ellipse," was built as "a part ellipse inboard of the trilithon ellipse and more or less concentric to it" (Heath 15). There were once nineteen tall and slender bluestone stones facing northeast within the innermost construction which formed a "U" shape that marked the nineteen year cycle of the moon and the sun, a construction that closely resembles the "U" shape of the Bucrania at the Knossos temple-complex. Likewise, in Scotland, other Bronze Age monuments marked the nineteen year cycle on their stones. At Caithness just south of Loch Stemster in an area of heather and peat is a megalithic horseshoe that is aligned to the major and minor standstills of the nineteen year cycle of the moon and the sun (Burl 121). And in the Outer Hebrides at Callanish are the remains of what was a "cove" or "U" shape of stones surrounded by two concentric circles, the whole of which resembles the construction of The Bluestone Ellipse at Stonehenge (Ponting 18).

Although much research is yet to be done on these ancient monuments, it is evident that the peoples of the Bronze Age had an abundance of information as time keepers of the night sky. In the Iron Age, the information from the stone circles, the stone horseshoes and "U" formations, and the massive Bucrania, is transferred to "modern" forms in much the same way we have transferred information from our books to the computer and the internet. In Greece by the fifth century BC, Meton of Athens, a renowned mathematician and astronomer, devised a luni-solar calendar using a fixed system of recording astronomical observations that was based on the nineteen year cycle of the moon and the sun. He called his device a parapegma, and to this day, the nineteen year cycle is referred to as the Metonic Cycle. Tablets of bronze that recorded the nineteen year cycle were arranged as a calendar for the people, and they were erected in the center of Athens in 432 BC. The calendar was called "The Cycle of Golden Numbers" because the bronze or golden characters that were etched in the tablets glowed inside the temple in which they were placed. The Metonic Calendar used months of 29 and 30 days as well as intercalary months to balance the cycles of the moon and the sun in the nineteen years. Every nineteen years, it was turned over and repeated itself to continue the cycle through infinite time.

The parapegma was named as such because it had movable pegs and an inscription to indicate the approximate correspondence between the risings of the moon with a solar date. It could be adjusted as necessary for the cycle of the moon and the sun to coincide, and it marked the primary stars that rise in the northeast each month. Even though the pattern of the overall tablet was based on the nineteen year cycle, the parapegma also predicted the movement of the stars, the planets and the eclipse cycles. Four parapegmas have been discovered thus far. The first is the one in Athens attributed to Meton. The second and the third parapegmas to be discovered were dated to the second century and the early first century BC. They were excavated at Miletus, which is in present day Turkey, and they were both made of stone. These stone calendars or parapegmata that were displayed for public use also had a list of star phases and eclipse predictions as well as the repeating nineteen year cycle of the moon and the sun. By the second century AD, the Alexandrian astronomer, Claudius Ptolemy included such a calendar in his *Phases of the Fixed Stars and Collection of Weather Signs*, thus introducing the calendar into a written text (Taub 1). The fourth and final parapegma that has been discovered thus far is the bronze tablet unearthed in a vineyard in Coligny, France that dates to the first century BC called The Coligny Calendar; it, too, is based on the nineteen year cycle with markings for the stars and eclipses.

The Coligny Calendar has recently been translated by a group of scholars, one of which is I, in an effort to revive the cycles of the moon, the sun and the stars for people today. We have re-named our translation of the calendar The Sequani Calendar in honor of the Sequani tribe of Celts in whose territory it was found. After discovering that the calendar is based on the nineteen year cycle of the moon and the sun, and that the cycle begins and is oriented to the rising of the moon and its relation to the constellation Taurus at the Winter Solstice, our translation of the calendar was begun again in 2001. As a daily calendar, it reveals the exact phase of the moon, the nutation cycle of the moon, the stars that are rising in the northeast at dusk, the corresponding solar date and, most importantly, the pattern of the moon and the sun in the nineteen year cycle. Here, the moon is measured in relation to the constellation of the Taurus, the Bull. Like the measurements of the Bucrania, the phases of the moon are also measured on The Sequani Calendar in relation to the constellations that are in proximity to Taurus: Aldebaran and the Pleiades. Then, the phase of the moon is measured in relation to where it resides in The

Horns of the Bull; again, in the ninth year, the moon jumps The Horns of the Bull. The measurement of the full moon in The Horns of Consecration at the Winter Solstice is the most important measurement on The Sequani Calendar, as it is in the measurements used by the Minoan-Mycenaean culture, because this is close to where the galactic equator meets the ecliptic.

The numerology of these calendars is based on the Winter Solstice as a focal point. Like the moon in its darkest phase, the sun at the Winter Solstice has reached the depths of the Underworld below the horizon and is now ready to resurrect into a new life and rise again into a new cycle. It is ready to regenerate into another cycle, drawing from the energies of the moon and the sun for its strength at this time. This moment is represented on the designs on the robe of the astronomer priestesses at Knossos, on the designs of the walls at Knowth at Newgrange in Ireland, and in the poetry of the Celtic Bards. In the moment, the sacrifice of the bull where his energies in the form of his blood are poured into the roots of the World Tree, connects the moment of regeneration, continuity and renewal of the earth and all its forms to the heavens. Moreover, it also marks the beginning of a new nineteen year cycle of which three cycles most likely represented the lifetime of the ancients. In a comprehensive sense, the ancients were able to keep track of their own lives and their ability to renew their energies by drawing down the energies of the heavenly bodies. Time keepers were not just astronomers, but messengers of the divine forces, and calendars were much more than dates on a page. The Coligny Calendar, a calendar of the Druids of the Sequani tribe in the first century BC, was the last to keep track of time in this manner before the forces of Julius Caesar conquered the tribe and installed the new Roman calendar that used only solar time.

Fortunately, the calendar of the Druids containing information from as far back as the Paleolithic and Neolithic cultures, was buried in a vineyard in order that the Romans would not discover it. Although the same information was recorded on the stones, the calendar was the "modern" and accessible representation of the information. Since it has been unearthed, the mythologies and the divine meaning of the cycles on which the calendar is based have been revealed. Primarily, the nineteen year cycle is the guiding cycle of the three cycles of an average lifetime. The revelation of the meaning behind the cycles came from a primary star that is identified at the beginning of each month on the calendar. Because the name of the primary stars come to us from the Greeks, the deities first revealed themselves through the Iron Age mythology of the Greeks. The pattern of the year, now fully explicated in our book, *The Myth of the Year: Returning to the Origin of the Druid Calendar*, (Lanham, Maryland: University Press of America, 2003), follows the patterns of the Eleusinian Mysteries in the Fall, The Horns of Consecration or the

Horns of Taurus in the Winter, the sacrifice of the bull or The Dionysian Mysteries in the Spring, and the Mother Goddess in the Summer. Basically, there are several primary stars for each season that identify the pattern in the sky in terms of a group of constellations that tell the story of each season.

Like the Greek calendars, the parapegmata, the ancient stone circles containing the "U" formation such as Stonehenge, and the Bucrania of the Minoan-Mycenaean civilization, the Coligny Calendar uses moon cycles of 30 and 29 alternately and an intercalary moon to keep the nineteen year cycles of the moon and the sun in perfect coordination. The logistics of these ancient time keepers seem to utilize the same astronomy in terms of the stars and the patterns of the planets as well, but this information is yet to be revealed to us. However, the patterns of the year and the nineteen year cycle are our current guides. They have revealed the underlying meaning of the seasons and the cycles of the celestial as the ancients knew them in connection with the earth and our own human cycles. Festivals are celebrated, holy nights are marked and the meaning of time becomes relevant as a circular process of renewal and rejuvenation of which we become an active participant. Most notably, the changes, such as the addition of an intercalary moon every two and one half years, and the measurement of the full moon in The Horns of Consecration every nineteen years, not to mention the intricate adjustments of the planets and the eclipses as well as those adjustments that follow the patterns of the stars over thousands of years, are yet to be fully understood.

Moreover, other cultures, such as the Egyptian and the Native American cultures have yet to be included in the study of the archetype of the nineteen year cycle of The Goddess and the Bull. Notably, in the Egyptian Dynasty of Sethi 1st in the thirteenth century BC, the nineteenth dynasty of ancient Egypt, a ceiling fresco in the tomb of Sethi 1st depicts nineteen gods and one goddess, presumably Isis, approaching a bull with eleven deities on the left and nine deities on the right. Each deity holds a full moon on her or his head; the eighteenth deity holds his moon in a Bucrania. According to Jean Louis Pagé, the message of the fresco states: "After many generations, a time will come where the sacred words of the West will be revealed and reunited with the messages from the Orient within a divine work." This "divine work" will be produced in 1999 and 2001 (213–17). Interesting as Pagé's theory may seem, the fact that the fresco represents the nineteen year cycle of the sun and the moon and the fact that a bull is at its center is at least explicit. Pagé also describes a fresco in the tomb of Sethi 1st that is called "The Sacred Ox." Here, concludes Pagé, the same message is stated a different way (231–32). Again, it is assumed that whether the message of futuristic prediction is valid or not, the bull, known as the deity of Apis, and the moon known as Chons and Thoth to the Egyptians, is a dominant force in their mythology.

An interesting tale in the Native American mythology of the Blackfoot tribe of the Great Plains, which is tellingly close to the myths of The Goddess and the Bull in the Mediterranean and Europe, as well as the great "U' formation at Chimney Rock, Colorado which measures the nutation cycle of the moon, might prove that the Native Americans have a similar archetype as The Goddess and the Bull in their culture. In the Blackfoot tale, a young woman promises to marry a buffalo to increase the herds and relieve the cycle of hunger and deprivation for her people. One large bull takes her up on her promise leading her into the prairie. Like the hieros gamos, the woman mates with the buffalo, and when her father comes to find her and is stamped by the buffalo, the buffalo tells the woman that now she knows what it is like to be sacrificed for the people. He tells her if she can bring her father back to life, he will allow her to return to her tribe and start a new cycle of abundance and wealth with the buffalo as their prime source of food. The woman revives her father, and the new cycle begins. The buffalo says to her: "' We shall now teach you our dance and our song. You must never forget it, because it contains the secret of the reincarnation of those of us who are killed by men for our flesh'" (Hirsch 350).

The Buffalo Dance of the Blackfoot has similar characteristics to the worship of The Goddess and the Bull in the Minoan-Mycenaean culture where the goddess and the bull have the hieros gamos, the bull is sacrificed for the regeneration of a new cycle, and the goddess or the woman learns the secrets of eternal life through sacrifice. The Buffalo Dance, like the Geranos, or crane dance of the ancient Minoans and Greeks, is reminiscent of the dance with the bull that symbolizes the dance of life and death, of renewal and regeneration itself. The woman in the Blackfoot myth even uses a bird as her helper. Perhaps, the dance eventually becomes the dance of war in the Iron Age where the goddess, woman or queen must continue the cycle of sacrifice and renewal through sacrificing her tribe, like Maeve does in the Táin. When the imagery of The Goddess and the Bull disappears in the Iron Age in Europe and the Mediterranean, only in a culture once removed from the discovery of modern warfare, such as the Native American culture, is the motive for the sacrifice retained in the face of the eventually encroaching patriarchy. Fortunately, peoples such as the Blackfoot, are still in existence bringing ancient customs to light. What we, as a culture, have to do then, in European and Mediterranean based civilization, is to unearth the past, using tools such as The Sequani Calendar, the mythology, and the archeoastronomy of our ancestors to re-vitalize our own culture which has left the knowledge of the cycles of the heavenly bodies, the knowledge of the moon, the sun, the planets, and the stars buried for eons.

Perhaps, a recent discovery will serve as a symbol for future generations to realize the intelligence with which our ancestors approached the study of the heavens. This year, the rebuilding of the Antikythera Device, an advanced calendar which records the nineteen year cycle of the moon and the sun, the phases of stars, and the movements of the five visible planets, was accomplished by several scientists who became aware of the significance of this ancient time keeper from the first century BC. The Antikythera Device, which is a mechanism or calendrical device discovered from a shipwreck off the coast of the island of Antikythera in the Mediterranean, is an amazing machine of gears and wheels that determines the measurements of the celestial bodies over thousands of years. The cycles it measures attest to the sophistication of the ancient astronomers in their quest to understand the heavens. The whole purpose of the Antikythera Device was to mechanize the cyclic relations of the bodies of the night sky in order, not only to understand astronomy and navigation of the seas, but to establish a relation between those bodies and human efforts. The connection to the starry dynamo is a connection that speaks to the practicality of living on earth and realizing the effect the celestial has on humankind, but it is also one that speaks to the our spirit.

The study of the archetype of The Goddess and the Bull, which dates back to the beginning of our efforts to keep time in the Paleolithic Era, is a journey through time and culture. In an effort to establish a cycle of the moon and the sun where the cosmos demonstrates its continuity through eternity, we have grasped the infinite and made it our own. We have imagined it as a goddess, a mother figure who is symbolic of the cycles of birth and death. Her names are many and her forms varied. And the energy that the goddess requires to continue the cycles of life has been imagined as a bull, a fertile and virile force of nature that is seen in the sky as the Winter Solstice constellation of Taurus. The movement of the celestial bodies has been captured as our own, and the sacrifice we offer of the bull verifies our appreciation of the infinite cycles of which we briefly participate. The energies of The Goddess and the Bull are transformed by us in order that we realize our part in the eternal cycles of life. To frame that in human and animal terms, in symbols and metaphors of the infinite, gives us the strength to believe in the eternal return. Moreover, it connects the earth, the heavens, the world of the dead, and our own world into one viable schemata of which we become an active participant. Revitalizing that participation in the infinite may only open the doors of perception once again.

Appendix I

The Lunar Months

Greek Attic Calendar	Celtic Sequani Calendar
Hekatombaion	Simivisonnios
Metageitnion	Equos
Boedromion	Elembivious
Pyanopsion	Edrinios
Maimakerion	Cantlos
Poseidon	Samonios
Gamelion	Dumannios
Anthesterion	Rivros
Elaphebolion	Anagantios
Mounychion	Ogronios
Thargelian	Cutios
Skiraphorion	Giamonios

Appendix II

Count the 19 year cycles. See explanation at end.
Don't add intercalary 30 nights.
12/22 2001 to 12/11 2002 5th year and 1st year 355 nights 58th and 1st year

2001 to 12/22 355	20819	end w/4th	50 moons
		add 1	
		night	

365 −11 nights in 2001 1/2 2001 to 12/21 2001 354 nights   6940

2000	366 nights	20465	3rd	

1 + 366 + 18 in 1999 12/14 1999 to 1/1 2001 for 385 nights

1999	365	20080	2nd	

347 + 6 nights in 1998 12/26 1998 to 12/13 1999 for 353 nights

1998	365	19727	1st	

359 + 26 nights in 1997 12/6 1997 to 12/25 1998 for 385 nights

1997	365	19342	5th	62 moons

339 + 16 nights in 1996 12/16 1996 to 12/5 1997 for 355 nights

1996	366	18987	4th	

350 + 3 nights in 1995 12/29 1995 to 12/15 1996 for 353 nights

1995	365	18634	3rd	

362 + 22 nights in 1994 12/9 1994 to 12/28 1995 for 385 nights

1994	365	18249	2nd	

342 + 11 nights in 1993 12/21 1993 to 12/8 1994 for 353 nights

1993	365	17896	1st	

354 + 31 nights in 1992 12/1 1992 to 12/20 1993 for 385 nights

1992	366	17511	5th	62 moons

335 +20 nights in 1991 12/12 1991 to 11/30 1992 for 355 nights

1991	365	17156	4th	

345 + 8 nights in 1990 12/24 1990 to 12/11 1991 for 353 nights

1990	365	16803	3rd	

357 + 28 nights in 1989 12/4 1989 to 12/23 1990 for 385 nights

1989   365   16418   2nd
337 + 16 nights in 1988 12/16 1988 to 12/3 1989 for 353 nights
1988   366   16065   1st
350 + 35 nights in 1987 11/27 1987 to 12/15 1988 for 385 nights

1987   365   15680   5th   61 moons
330 + 25 nights in 1986 12/7 1986 to 11/26 1987 for 355 nights
1986   365   15325   4th
340 + 13 nights in 1985 12/19 1985 to 12/6 1986 for 353 nights
1985   365   14972   3rd
352 + 33 nights in 1984 11/29 1984 to 12/18 1985 for 385 nights
1984   366   14587   2nd
333 + 20 nights in 1983 12/12 1983 to 11/28 1984 for 353 nights
1983   365   14234   1st
345 + 10 nights in 1982 12/22 1982 to 12/11 1983 for 355 nights
first year is also 5th year this cycle start 3rd cycle

end w/4th
1982   365   13879   4th   50 moons
355 - 2 nights in 1982 1/3 1982 to 12/21 1982 for 353 nights
1981   365   13526   3rd
2 + 365 + 18 in 1980 12/14 1980 to 1/2 1982 for 385 nights
1980   366   13141   2nd
348 + 5 nights 1979 12/27 1979 to 12/13 1980 for 353 nights
1979   365   12788   1st
360 + 25 nights in 1978 12/7 1978 to 12/26 1979 for 385 nights

1978   365   12403   5th   62 moons
340 + 15 nights in 1977 12/17 1977 to 12/6 1978 for 355 nights
1977   365   12048   4th
350 + 3 nights in 1976 12/29 1976 to 12/16 1977 for 353 nights
1976   366   11695   3rd
363 + 22 nights in 1975 12/10 1975 to 12/28 1976 for 385 nights
1975   365   11310   2nd
343+ 10 nights in 1974 12/22 1974 to 12/9 1975 for 353 nights
1974   365   10957   1st
355 + 30 nights in 1973 12/2 1973 to 12/21 1974 for 385 nights

1973   365   10572   5th   62 moons
335 + 20 nights in 1972 12/12 1972 to 12/1 1973 for 355 nights
1972   366   10217   4th
346 + 7 nights in 1971 12/25 1971 to 12/11 1972 for 353 nights
1971   365   9864   3rd
358 + 27 nights in 1970 12/5 1970 to 12/24 1971 for 385 nights
1970   365   9479   2nd
338 + 15 nights in 1969 12/17 1969 to 12/4 1970 for 353 nights
1969   365   9126   1st
350 + 35 nights in 1968 11/27 1968 to 12/16 1969 for 385 nights

1968 366 8741 5th 61 moons
331 + 24 nights in 1967 12/8 1967 to 11/26 1968 for 355 nights
1967 365 8386 4th
341 + 12 nights in 1966 12/20 1966 to 12/7 1967 for 353 nights
1966 365 8033 3rd
354 + 32 nights in 1965 11/30 1965 to 12/19 1966 for 385 nights
1965 365 7648 2nd
333 + 20 nights in 1964 12/12 1964 to 11/29 1965 for 353 nights
1964 366 7295 1st
346 + 9 nights in 1963 12/23 1963 to 12/11 1964 for 355 nights
start second cycle
end w/ 4th year 5th year and 1st year are the same

1963 365 6940 4th add 1 This stretch is
night 50 moons
356 −2 night in 1963 1/3 1963 to 12/22 1963 for 354 nights
1962 365 6586 3rd
4 + 365 +18 nights in 1961 12/14 1961 to 1/2 1963 for 385 nights
1961 365 6201 2nd
347 + 6 nights in 1960 12/26 1960 to 12/13 1961 for 353 nights
1960 366 5848 1st
360 + 25 nights in 1959 12/7 1959 to 12/25 1960 for 385 nights

1959 365 5463 5th this stretch is
62 moons
340 + 15 nights in 1958 12/17 1958 to 12/6 1959 for 355 nights
1958 365 5108 4th
350 + 3 nights in 1957 12/29 1957 to 12/16 1958 for 353 nights

1957 365 4755 3rd
362 + 23 nights in 1956 12/9 1956 to 12/28 1957 for 385 nights
1956 366 4370 2nd
343 + 10 nights in 1955 12/22 1955 to 12/8 1956 for 353 nights
1955 365 4017 1st
355 + 30 nights in 1954 12/2 1954 to 12/21 1955 for 385 nights

1954 365 3632 5th 62 moon
335 + 20 nights in 1953 12/12 1953 to 12/1 1954 for 355 nights
1953 365 3277 4th
345 + 8 nights in 1952 12/24 1952 to 12/11 1953 for 353 nights
1952 366 2924 3rd
358 + 27 nights in 1951 12/5 1951 to 12/23 1952 for 385 nights
1951 365 2539 2nd
338 + 15 nights in 1950 12/17 1950 to 12/4 1951 for 353 nights
1950 365 2186 1st
350 + 35 nights in 1949 11/27 1949 to 12/16 1950 for 385 nights

1949 365 1801 5th 61 moons
330 + 25 nights in 1948 12/7 1948 to 11/26 1949 for 355 nights

1948   366   1446   4th
341 + 12 nights in 1947 12/20 1947 to 12/6 1948 for 353 nights
1947   365   1093   3rd
353 + 32 nights in 1946 11/30 1946 to 12/19 1947 for 385 nights
1946   365   708   2nd
333 + 20 nights in 1945 12/12 1945 to 11/29 1946 for 353 nights

1945   365   355   1st
345 + 10 nights in 1944 12/22 1944 to 12/11 1945 for 355 nights
start first cycle
5th year and 1st year are the same This is also 58th year and 1st year
This chart reconciles the Sun and Moon and the Bull's Horns with the winter solstice
over the 19 year mythological standard. It takes 3 cycles for this to work out; however
there is little correction needed in a nineteen year period, 1 night every other 19. The
counting starts at the end.
Metonic Cycle 6939.6
precession is a year and a day.

6940 + 6939 + 6940 + 20819
solar count 20819 divided by 365.2422 = 57
lunar count 20819 divided by 29.53059027 = 705

The first quarter moon backs itself up from the solstice. There is notice of this. By the
time the first quarter moon, in intervals of 58 years, is at December 25, an intercalary
can be added previous.

Appendix III

Moon in the Horns of the Bull

	WS	IMBOLG	SEQ	BELTAIN	SOLS	LUGNA	FEQ	SAM
	see Bull East rising sunset	see Bull up sunset E	see Bull West at sunset sets at midnight	see Bull set right after Sun 8:45 PM	see Bull rising out of Sun AM only	see Bull rising 2:30 AM AZM 63 sunrise AZM 65	see Bull rising 10:30 PM AZM 59 note WS	see Bull rising 8:15 PM NE
2001	1st QTR sets 11 pm AZM 255 Sat in BH	1st QTR crosses through BH 2-3 and 2-4 waxing	3rd QTR	1st QTR 4-30 in Can	New TE see Moon & BH 6-19	Full 8-4 Sat in BH	3rd QTR in Sag Sat in BH	Full Sat in BH straight through BH by 11-13
2002	2 nights from Full on 19th AZM 61 rising	1-28 Full 3rd QTR on 2-4	1st QTR through BH 3-19 to 3-21	5-3 3rd QTR in Cap Full 4-26 see Sat & Mars in BH	Full 6-24 top of Sag	3rd QTR	Full 9-21	25 nights old New on 11-4
2003	2 nights from New	New 1 night old on sunset side	Full 3-17 next to Coma Berenices	New thin crescent in BH 5-3	3rd QTR by Pisces AM	1st QTR	New 9-25	1st QTR in Capricorn

WS	IMBOLG	SEQ	BELTAIN	SOLS	LUGNA	F EQ	SAM
2004 Full 12-25 up passes BH as BH rises	*2004* 1st QTR 1-28 11 nights old slide by BH	*2004* New	*2004* 12 nights old with Coma Berenices Full on 5-4	*2004* 1st QTR by Coma Berenices	*2004* Full 7-31 AZM123 in PM	*2004* 10 nights old Full with Pisces 9-27	*2004* 18 nights old top side of BH total eclipse 10-27 Full
2005 3rd QTR 12-24 by Coma Berenices Crosses due East	*2005* 3rd QTR 2-2 due East AM	*2005* 1st QTR 3-17 slides by BH Full 3-25 by Coma Berenices	*2005* 3rd QTR 4-30 by Cap	*2005* Full AZM 132 above Sag	*2005* 3rd QTR 7-28 8-1 AM 25 nights E of BH AZM 59	*2005* 3rd QTR slides by BH	*2005* New on 11-1
2006 New setting AZM 232 after sun	*2006* 1st QTR 2-4 Moon with Mars & Pleiades passes top of BH	*2006* 20 nights old Full with ecl on 3-14 3rd QTR 3-22 with Sag	*2006* New on 4-27 side of BH 4-29 & 5-1 thin crescent	*2006* 3rd QTR thin crescent slides by BH 6-24	*2006* 1st QTR with Jupiter	*2006* 2 nights from New	*2006* 10 nights old Full on 11-4 top side of BH
2007 Full 12-23 through	*2007* Full in Cancer rising	*2007* 2 nights old New 3-24	*2007* Full between Spica	*2007* 1st QTR	*2007* Full 7-29 AZM 121	*2007* Full 9-26	*2007* 3rd QTR on 11-1

(continued)

WS	IMBOLG	SEQ	BELTAIN	SOLS	LUGNA	F EQ	SAM
BH with Mars	passed BH to the E	passes by BH at 1st QTR	& Libra		8-1 18 nights old AZM 97 9:27 PM		
2008 23 nights old 2 nights from 3rd QTR	2008 3rd QTR 1-29	2008 Full 3-21 next to Spica	2008 4 nights to New on 5-5	2008 Full top of Sag	2008 New on 7-31	2008 3rd QTR 9-21 9-23 24 nights old	2008 3 nights from New
2009 2 nights from 1st QTR	2009 1st QTR 2-2 passes left of BH	2009 3rd QTR above Sag	2009 1st QTR by Can	2009 New on 6-22	2009 1st QTR 7-28	2009 2 nights from 1st QTR close to Antares	2009 Full on 11-1 top side of BH through 11-15
2010 Full on 12-20 slide by top of BH	2010 Full 1-29 slides right of BH 1-25	2010 1st QTR slides through top BH 3-22	2010 Full on 4-28 AZM 118	2010 1st QTR on 6-18 Full on 6-25	2010 3rd QTR E of BH AM 8-5 thin crescent top of BH	2010 Full on 9-22	2010 3rd QTR on 10-30
2011 3rd QTR 12-17 New on 12-25	2011 2 nights to New waning sliver	2011 Full next to Coma Berenices	2011 New 3 nights old right in BH	2011 3rd QTR 6-22 in in BH 6-29	2011 2 nights old AZM 270 twilight 7-26	2011 3rd QTR 9-20 through BH to	2011 1st QTR on 11-12

WS	IMBOLG	SEQ	BELTAIN	SOLS	LUGNA	F EQ	SAM
	↑rises ½ hour before sun	on 3-19			crescent in BH AM	the top	
2012 9 nights old 2 nights after 1st QTR	*2012* 1st QTR jumps BH 2-2 but not centered	*2012* New on 3-22	*2012* 10 nights old 1st QTR 4-28	*2012* New on 6-19	*2012* Full 7:16 PM AZM 110	*2012* 2 nights after 1st QTR	*2012* 2 nights past Full with Jup inside BH 11-1
2013 Full on 12-17 low side of BH 3rd QTR 12-25	*2013* 3rd QTR 2-3 rises 12:46 AM AZM 116	*2013* 1st QTR 3-19 with Jup in BH 3-17	*2013* 3rd QTR 5-2	*2013* Full on 6-24	*2013* thin crescent edge of BH AM 3rd QTR 7-29 New 8-6	*2013* 20 nights old right in BH 3rd QTR 9-26	*2013* New 11-3
2014 New	*2014* New	*2014* Full 3-16 3rd QTR 3-23	*2014* New 3 nights old moves through BH 5-1 & 5-2	*2014* 3rd QTR on 6-19	*2014* 5 nights old 1st QTR 8-3 by Spica & Mars	*2014* New	*2014* 1st QTR 10-30 in Cap 11-8 moon 17 nights low side of BH (continued)

WS	IMBOLG	SEQ	BELTAIN	SOLS	LUGNA	F EQ	SAM
2015 Full 12-25 W of BH	*2015* Full 2-3 passed BH 1-28	*2015* New	*2015* Full 5-2 by by Spica	*2015* 1st QTR 6-23	*2015* Full 7-30 AZM 111 6:58 PM	*2015* 10 nights old Full on 9-27 TE	*2015* 10-28 17 nights low side of BH 10-31 2 nights to 3rd QTR
2016 3rd QTR	*2016* 3rd QTR 1-31	*2016* Full next to Regulas	*2016* 1 night past 3rd QTR	*2016* Full 6-19 3rd QTR	*2016* New	*2016* 3rd QTR 9-22 low side of BH	*2016* 1 night past New
2017 3 nights from New setting after Sun	*2017* 2 nights to 1st QTR	*2017* 3rd QTR with Sat between Sag & Sco	*2017* 1st QTR by Can	*2017* 1st QTR by Can	*2017* 10 nights old Full 8-7 AZM 110	*2017* 4 nights old 1st Qtr 9-27 at top of Sag	*2017* 11 nights old 1st QTR Cap 11-4 low side BH
2018 Full exact in BH with Aldebaran	*2018* Full on 1-30	*2018* 4 nights old 1st QTR jump BH between 3-21 & 3-23	*2018* Full 4-30	*2018* 1st QTR 6-19	*2018* Full 7-27 at BH 8-6 AM	*2018* Full 9-24	*2018* 3rd QTR Can

WS	IMBOLG	SEQ	BELTAIN	SOLS	LUGNA	F EQ	SAM
2019 New 12-25 Moon before sun by Spica & Mars 3rd QTR 12-18	*2019* New 2-4 passing Jup & Ven	*2019* Full next to Coma Berenices	*2019* New 5-4	*2019* New on 6-20	*2019* New on 7-31 thin cres setting right after sun with Mars	*2019* 3rd QTR 9-22 passing through BH	*2019* 4 nights old with Jup Sat above
2020 1st QTR	*2020* 1st QTR through BH 2-3 & 2-4 good leap through BH	*2020* 3rd QTR twilight Antares nice line of Mars Sat & Mer	*2020* 1st QTR 4-30 next to Can	*2020* New	*2020* Full 8-2 AZM 122	*2020* 3rd QTR 9-23	*2020* Full on 10-31 close to Full through BH

AZM   azimuth calculated for Elkins, WV and times indicated EST

GLOSSARY FOR APPENDIX 2

BH	Taurus
Can	Cancer
Cap	Capricorn
cres	crescent
E	east
ecl	eclipse
F EQ	fall equinox
IMBOLG	winter cross quarter day*
Jup	Jupiter
LUGNA	summer cross quarter day* Lugnasad
Mer	Mercury
Sag	Sagittarius
SAM	fall cross quarter day* Samhain
Sat	Saturn
Sco	Scorpio
SEQ	spring equinox
SOLS	summer solstice
TE	total eclipse
Ven	Venus
WS	winter solstice

*Cross quarter days charted by traditional Celtic cross quarter days: February 1, May 1, August 1 and November 1.

Works Cited

CHAPTER ONE

Brennan, Martin. *The Stones of Time*. Rochester, Vermont: Inner Traditions, 1994.

Burl, Aubrey. *A Guide to the Stone Circles of Britain, Ireland, and Britain*. New Haven: Yale University Press, 1995.

Cameron, D.O. *Symbols of Birth and Death in the Neolithic Era*. London: Kenyon-Deane, Ltd., 1981.

Campbell, Joseph. "And We Washed Our Weapons in the Sea: Gods and Goddesses of the Neolithic Period" Program 3, Vol. I, Tape II. *Transformations of Myth Through Time*. Public Media Video, 1989.

Gimbutas, Marija. *The Goddesses and Gods of Old Europe: Myths and Cult Images*. Berkeley: University of California Press, 1982.

——. *The Language of the Goddess: Unearthing the Hidden Symbols of Western Civilization*. New York: Thames and Hudson, 1989.

——. *The Living Goddesses*. Edited and Supplemented by Miriam Robbins Dexter. Berkeley/ Los Angeles: University of California Press, 1999.

Hawkins, Gerald S. *Stonehenge Decoded*. New York: Dell Publishing, 1978.

Heath, Robin. *Sun, Moon, and Stonehenge*. Cardigan, Wales: Bluestone Press, 1998.

Leroi-Gourhan, André. *Treasures of Prehistoric Art*. New York: Harry Abrams, 1967.

Mellaart, James. "Çatal Hüyük and Anatolian Kilims" *The Goddess of Anatolia*. Volume II. Adenau, West Germany: Eskenazi, 1989.

Murphy, Anthony. "Astronomical Significance of Kerb 51 at Dowth" *Mythical Ireland*. 4 November 2004 <http://mythicalireland.com/>.

Ransome, Hilda. *The Sacred Bee in Ancient Times and Folklore*. Boston: Houghton Mifflin, 1937.

Ridpath, Ian, Editor. *Norton's Star Atlas and Reference Handbook*. Edinburgh Gate, England: Longman, 1998.

West, Anthony. *Serpent in the Sky: The High Wisdom of Ancient Egypt*. New York: Julian Press, 1987.

Wood, John Edwin. *Sun, Moon and Standing Stones*. Oxford: Oxford University Press, 1978.

Yeats, William Butler. *A Vision*. London: MacMillan, 1974.

CHAPTER TWO

Baring, Anne and Jules Cash. *The Myth of the Goddess*. New York: Penguin, 1991.

Evans, Sir Arthur. *The Palace of Minos: A Comparative Account of the Successive Stages of the Early Cretan Civilization as Illustrated By the Discoveries*. Vols. I–IV. New York: Biblo and Tannen, 1964.

Gimbutas, Marija. *The Goddesses and Gods of Old Europe: Myths and Cult Images*. Berkeley: Univ.of California Press, 1996.

——. *The Living Goddesses*, Edited and Supplemented by Miriam Robbins Dexter. Berkeley: Univ. of California Press, 1999.

Griaule, Marcel. *Conversations with Ogotemmeli: An Introduction to Dogon Religious Ideas*. Oxford: Oxford Univ. Press, 1965.

Graves, Robert. *The Greek Myths*. Vols. I-II. New York: Penguin, 1960.

Karetsou, Alexandra. "The Peak Sanctuary of Mt. Juktas" *Sanctuaries and Cults in the Aegean Bronze Age: Proceedings of the First International Symposium at the Swedish Institute in Athens 12–13 August, 1980*, Eds. Robin Hägg and Nanno Marinatos. Athens: Almquist and Wiksel, 1980.

Logiadou-Platonos, Sosso. *Knossos: The Minoan Civilization*. Athens: Mathioulakis & Co., 2006.

Morford, Mark P.O. and Robert J. Lenardon. *Classical Mythology*. New York: Oxford Univ. Press, 2007.

Nilsson, Martin P. *Minoan-Mycenaean Religion and its Survival in The Greek Religion*. New York: Biblo and Tannen, 1949.

CHAPTER THREE

Burkert, Walter. *Greek Religion*. Cambridge: Harvard Univ. Press, 1985.

Butler, Alan. *The Bronze Age Computer Disc*. London: Quantum, 1999.

Eliade, Mircea. *The Myth of the Eternal Return, or Cosmos and History*. Princeton: Princeton Univ. Press, 1974.

Evans, Sir Arthur. *The Palace of Minos: A Comparative Account of the Successive Stages of the Early Cretan Civilization as Illustrated By the Discoveries*. Vols. I-IV. New York: Biblo and Tannen, 1964.

Gimbutas, Marija. *The Goddesses and Gods of Old Europe: Myths and Cult Images*. Berkeley: Univ. of California Press, 1996.

Godart, Louis and Yannis Tzedaris. "The Bull in the Minoan-Mycenaean World" *The Bull in the Mediterranean World: Myths and Cults*. Athens: Hellenic Ministry of Culture, Hellenic Cultural Organization SA and Cultural Olympiad 2001–2004, 2003: 73–6.

Graves, Robert. *The Greek Myths.* Vols. I-II. New York: Penguin, 1960.

Logiadou-Platonos, Sosso. *Knossos: The Minoan Civilization.* Athens: Mathioulakis & Co., 2006.

Nilsson, Martin P. *The Minoan-Mycenaean Religion and its Survival in Greek Religion.* New York: Biblo and Tannen, 1949.

Sakellarakis, J.A. *Musee D'Heracleion.* Athens: Ekdotike Athenon S.A., 1978.

CHAPTER FOUR

Benigni, Helen, Barbara Carter, and Eadhmonn Ua Cuinn. *The Myth of the Year: Returning to the Origin of the Druid Calendar.* Lanham: University Press of America, 2003.

Burkert, Walter. *Greek Religion.* Cambridge: Harvard University Press, 1985.

Burl, Aubrey. *A Guide to the Stone Circles of Britain, Ireland, and Brittany.* New Haven: Yale University Press, 1995.

Dexter, Miriam Robbins. "Queen Medb, Female Autonomy in Ancient Ireland, and Irish Matrilineal Traditions" *Proceedings of the Ninth Annual UCLA Indo-European Conference,* Edited by Karlene Jones-Bley, Angela Della Volpe, Miriam Robbins Dexter, and Martin E. Huld. Los Angeles: May 1997: 95–122.

Euripides. *Bakkhai.* Translated by Reginald Gibbons. Oxford: Oxford University Press, 2001.

Gimbutas, Marija. *The Living Goddesses.* Edited and Supplemented by Miriam Robbins Dexter. Berkeley/ Los Angeles: University of California Press, 1999.

Graves, Robert. *The Greek Myths.* New York: Penguin, 1960.

Heath, Robin. *Sun, Moon, and Stonehenge.* Cardigan, Wales: Bluestone Press, 1998.

Hirsch, Udo. *The Goddess From Anatolia.* Vol. III. Adenau: West Germany, Nava-Milano, 1989.

Kinsella, Thomas, Translator. *The Táin from the Irish epic Táin Bó Cuailnge.* Oxford: Oxford University Press, 1970.

Mackillop, James. *Oxford Dictionary of Celtic Mythology.* Oxford: Oxford University Press, 2000.

Matthews, John. *Taliesin: The Last Celtic Shaman.* Rochester, Vermont: Inner Traditions, 2002.

Murphy, Anthony and Richard Moore. *Island of the Setting Sun: In Search of Ireland's Ancient Astronomies.* Dublin: The Liffey Press, 2006.

Mylonas, George. *Eleusis and the Eleusinian Mysteries.* Princeton: Princeton University Press, 1972.

Nilsson, Martin P. *The Dionysiac Mysteries of the Hellenistic and Roman Age.* New York: Arno Press, 1975.

Ó Tuathail, Seán. "The Excellence of Ancient Word: Druid Rhetorics from Ancient Irish Tales." *Mythical Ireland,* Eds. Anthony Murphy and Richard Moore (1993) http://www.mythicalireland.com (1/27/2004).

Pagé, Jean Louis. *Atlantis Messages.* Québec: Les Éditions Zepheon Press, 2001.

Ponting, Gerald and Margaret Ponting. *The Stones Around Callanish*. Stornoway, Scotland: Stornoway Gazette, 1984.

Ross, Anne. *Pagan Celtic Britain*. Chicago: Academy Chicago Publishers, 1996.

Simon, Erika. *Festivals of Attica: An Archaeological Commentary*. Madison: University of Wisconsin Press, 1983.

Staal, Julius D.W. *New Patterns in the Sky: Myths and Legends of the Stars*. Blacksburg, Virginia: McDonald and Woodward, 1988.

Taub, Lisa and the Department of History and Philosophy of the University of Cambridge. "Ancient Weather Calendars" *Astronomy and Weather Predictions* (1999). http://www.hps.cam.ac.uk/starry/weather.html (1/29/2004).

Bibliography

Baring, Anne and Jules Cash. *The Myth of the Goddess*. New York: Penguin, 1991.

Benigni, Helen, Barbara Carter, and Eadhmonn Ua Cuinn. *The Myth of the Year: Returning to the Origin of the Druid Calendar*. Lanham: University Press of America, 2003.

Brennan, Martin. *The Stones of Time*. Rochester, Vermont: Inner Traditions, 1994.

Burkert, Walter. *Greek Religion*. Cambridge: Harvard Univ. Press, 1985.

Butler, Alan. *The Bronze Age Computer Disc*. London: Quantum, 1999.

Burl, Aubrey. *A Guide to the Stone Circles of Britain, Ireland, and Britain*. New Haven: Yale University Press, 1995.

Cameron, D.O. *Symbols of Birth and Death in the Neolithic Era*. London: Kenyon-Deane, Ltd., 1981.

Campbell, Joseph. "And We Washed Our Weapons in the Sea: Gods and Goddesses of the Neolithic Period" Program 3, Vol. I, Tape II. *Transformations of Myth Through Time*. Public Media Video, 1989.

Dexter, Miriam Robbins. "Queen Medb, Female Autonomy in Ancient Ireland, and Irish Matrilineal Traditions" *Proceedings of the Ninth Annual UCLA Indo-European Conference*, Edited by Karlene Jones-Bley, Angela Della Volpe, Miriam Robbins Dexter, and Martin E. Huld. Los Angeles: May 1997: 95–122.

Eliade, Mircea. *The Myth of the Eternal Return, or Cosmos and History*. Princeton: Princeton Univ. Press, 1974.

Evans, Sir Arthur. *The Palace of Minos: A Comparative Account of the Successive Stages of the Early Cretan Civilization as Illustrated By the Discoveries*. Vols. I-IV. New York: Biblo and Tannen, 1964.

Euripides. *Bakkhai*. Translated by Reginald Gibbons. Oxford: Oxford University Press, 2001.

Gimbutas, Marija. *The Goddesses and Gods of Old Europe: Myths and Cult Images*. Berkeley: University of California Press, 1982.

———. *The Language of the Goddess: Unearthing the Hidden Symbols of Western Civilization*. New York: Thames and Hudson, 1989.

———. *The Living Goddesses,* Edited and Supplemented by Miriam Robbins Dexter. Berkeley: University of California Press, 1999.

Godart, Louis and Yannis Tzedaris. "The Bull in the Minoan-Mycenaean World" *The Bull in the Mediterranean World: Myths and Cults.* Athens: Hellenic Ministry of Culture, Hellenic Cultural Organization SA and Cultural Olympiad 2001–2004, 2003: 73–6.

Griaule, Marcel. *Conversations with Ogotemmeli: An Introduction to Dogon Religious Ideas.* Oxford: Oxford Univ. Press, 1965.

Graves, Robert. *The Greek Myths.* Vols. I-II. New York: Penguin, 1960.

Hawkins, Gerald S. *Stonehenge Decoded.* New York: Dell Publishing, 1978.

Heath, Robin. *Sun, Moon, and Stonehenge.* Cardigan, Wales: Bluestone Press, 1998.

Hirsch, Udo. *The Goddess From Anatolia.* Vol. III. Adenau: West Germany, Nava-Milano, 1989.

Karetsou, Alexandra. "The Peak Sanctuary of Mt. Juktas" *Sanctuaries and Cults in the Aegean Bronze Age: Proceedings of the First International Symposium at the Swedish Institute in Athens 12–13 August, 1980,* Eds. Robin Hägg and Nanno Marinatos. Athens: Almquist and Wiksel, 1980.

Kinsella, Thomas, Translator. *The Táin from the Irish epic Táin Bó Cuailnge.* Oxford: Oxford University Press, 1970.

Leroi-Gourhan, André. *Treasures of Prehistoric Art.* New York: Harry Abrams, 1967.

Logiadou-Platonos, Sosso. *Knossos: The Minoan Civilization.* Athens: Mathioulakis & Co., 2006.

Mackillop, James. *Oxford Dictionary of Celtic Mythology.* Oxford: Oxford University Press, 2000.

Matthews, John. *Taliesin: The Last Celtic Shaman.* Rochester, Vermont: Inner Traditions, 2002.

Mellaart, James. "Çatal Hüyük and Anatolian Kilims" *The Goddess of Anatolia.* Volume II. Adenau, West Germany: Eskenazi, 1989.

Morford, Mark P.O. and Robert J. Lenardon. *Classical Mythology.* New York: Oxford Univ. Press, 2007.

Murphy, Anthony. "Astronomical Significance of Kerb 51 at Dowth" *Mythical Ireland.* 4 November 2004 http://mythicalireland.com/.

——— and Richard Moore. *Island of the Setting Sun: In Search of Ireland's Ancient Astronomies.* Dublin: The Liffey Press, 2006.

Mylonas, George. *Eleusis and the Eleusinian Mysteries.* Princeton: Princeton University Press, 1972.

Nilsson, Martin P. *Minoan-Mycenaean Religion and its Survival in The Greek Religion.* New York: Biblo and Tannen, 1949.

———. *The Dionysiac Mysteries of the Hellenistic and Roman Age.* New York: Arno Press, 1975.

Ó Tuathail, Seán. "The Excellence of Ancient Word: Druid Rhetorics from Ancient Irish Tales." *Mythical Ireland,* Eds. Anthony Murphy and Richard Moore (1993) http://www.mythicalireland.com (1/27/2004).

Pagé, Jean Louis. *Atlantis Messages.* Québec: Les Éditions Zepheon Press, 2001.

Ponting, Gerald and Margaret Ponting. *The Stones Around Callanish*. Stornoway, Scotland: Stornoway Gazette, 1984.

Ransome, Hilda. *The Sacred Bee in Ancient Times and Folklore*. Boston: Houghton Mifflin, 1937.

Ridpath, Ian, Editor. *Norton's Star Atlas and Reference Handbook*. Edinburgh Gate, England: Longman, 1998.

Ross, Anne. *Pagan Celtic Britain*. Chicago: Academy Chicago Publishers, 1996.

Sakellarakis, J.A. *Musee D'Heracleion*. Athens: Ekdotike Athenon S.A., 1978.

Simon, Erika. *Festivals of Attica: An Archeological Commentary*. Madison: University of Wisconsin Press, 1982.

Staal, Julius D.W. *New Patterns in the Sky: Myths and Legends of the Stars*. Blacksburg, Virginia: McDonald and Woodward, 1988.

Taub, Lisa and the Department of History and Philosophy of the University of Cambridge. "Ancient Weather Calendars" *Astronomy and Weather Predictions* (1999). http://www.hps.cam.ac.uk/starry/weather.html (1/29/2004).

West, Anthony. *Serpent in the Sky: The High Wisdom of Ancient Egypt*. New York: Julian Press, 1987.

Wood, John Edwin. *Sun, Moon and Standing Stones*. Oxford: Oxford University Press, 1978.

Yeats, William Butler. *A Vision*. London: MacMillan, 1974.

Index

Acropolis at Athens, 18
Acropolis at Mycenae, 21, 35
Aegina, island of Aphaia, 18, 24, 27, 31, 35
Aeschylus, 36
Agamemnon, tragedy of Aeschylus, 36
Agamemnon, the hero, 36
Agora, 18, 55
Ailill, Maeve's husband, 60–63
Aldebaran, star in Taurus, 39–40, 46, 67, 84
Amergin, Irish Bard, xv, 15, 51, 64–65
Amenemhêt, 37
Amnissos, cave of, 28
*Anthesteria,*Dionysian festival, 53. *See also* hieros gamos
Anthesterion, month of Greek calendar, 53–55, 73
Antikythera Device, xv, 52, 71
Aphaia, 18, 22, 24, 27, 31, 44
Apis, Egyptian bull deity, 69
Apollo, 13, 18
Aquarius, constellation, 27–28
Archon Basileus, 45
Arcturus, primary star of Boötes, 57
Ariadne, xiv, xv, 22, 24–27, 45, 55, 59
Aries, constellation, vii, 2
Artemis, 7, 13, 27
Asterius, 43

a-ta-na, title of the goddess, 24
Athana, 24
Athena, 23–24, 37
Attica, calendar of, 52–53, 90
"Atreus" Treasury, 42
Aubrey Holes, at Stonehenge, 11–12, 14, 90
Ayia Triada, 37, 45, 47

Bakkhai, Euripides' play, 54–56, 89, 91
Basilinna, or wife of Dionysus, 53, 55
Beltaine, 58–59
bile, Beltaine Tree, 59–60
Blackfoot tribe, Native American, 70
Bluestone Ellipse at Stonehenge, The, 14, 66
Boötes, constellation, 53, 55–57
Boscawen-Un, 13
Boukoleion, bull's stall, 55
Bouphonia, 52
Britomartis, xiv, 22, 27–28, 43–44, 54
Brú na Bóinne or Newgrange, 9–10
Buffalo Dance, of the Blackfoot Native American tribe, 70
Bull-grappling, 41–45, 53, 55

Caesar, Julius, 68
Caithness, 66
Callanish, 66, 90, 93

Carnac, 14, 19
Cassandra, 36
Cassiopeia, constellation, 38
Catal Hüyük, viii, 3–5, 7–9, 11, 14, 87, 92
Celestial North Pole, 38
Central Court at Knossos, 49
Ceridwen, Goddess of the Cauldron, 65
Chimney Rock, Colorado, 70
chiton, sacred robe, 37
Chrysalises, 29
Chthonic, xiv, 21–24, 40
City Dionysia, festival of Dionysus, 53, 55–56
Clytemnestra, 36
Coligny Calendar, xv–xvi, 52, 67–69
Coma Berenices, star cluster, 53–55, 81
Corinth, 31
Cornwall, 13, 19
Corona Borealis, constellation, 22, 25, 45, 53, 55
Cúchulainn, Celtic hero, 60–62, 64
Cup Bearer, Ganymedes, 28

Daedalus, 28, 44
Dartmoor, 13
Delphi, 18, 31, 49
Diktynna, 24
Diktyon or net, 28, 42
Diodorus Siculus, 12–13
Dionysus, xv, 24–25, 45, 51–57
Dipolieia, bull sacrifice, 52–53. *See also Bouphonia*
Diwija, Goddess, 48
Diwijeu, priest of Zeus, 48
Donn Cuailnge, the Brown Bull of Cuailnge, 60–63
Dorset Cursus, 13
Double Axe (s), The, 22, 24, 33, 35, 38, 40, 46–48, 52
Dowth at Newgrange, 9–10, 87, 92
Draco, constellation, 23
Druids, xv, 12, 58–59, 63, 65–66, 68, 95

Echidne, 29–30
Eclipse, 10, 12, 40, 67, 69, 81, 86
Ecliptic, 10, 39, 68

Eileithyia, xiv, 24, 27–28, 43, 54
Elaphebolion, Greek calendar month, 56–57, 73
Eleusinian Mysteries, 46, 63, 68, 89, 92
Erigone, Boötes' daughter, 56
Er-Lannic, 14
Eumaeus, swineherd in *Odyssey,* 58
Euripides, 54–56, 89, 91
Europa, viii, 43
Eurycleia, Odysseus' nurse, 58

Fergus, Maeve's lover, 61–62
Finnbennach, The White Bull of Connacht, 60, 62–63
Fir Bolg, Celtic crane bag, 59
Fresco of the Bull at Knossos, 45
Fual Medba, three dykes of Ireland, 60

Galactic equator, 39, 68
Gamelion, month of Greek calendar, 53, 73
Gerairai, Dionysian priestesses, 53, 56
Geranos or Crane Dance, 25–26, 70
Grand Stand Fresco at Knossos, 34
Grave Circle A at Mycenae, 33, 35–36
"Great Year", nineteen year cycle, 57–58
Griffin, 22, 28–30, 37

Haghia Triada, 26
Hall of the Double Axes at Knossos, 24
Hawthor, cow-goddess, viii, 37
Helius, sun deity, 44
Hera, viii, xiv, xv, 23, 35, 37, 48, 52, 56–57
Heraklion, viii, 21
Hieros Gamos, 24–27, 44, 48, 53, 55, 70. *See also* Sacred Marriage
Horns of the Bull, The, xiii, 4–5, 20, 34, 39–40, 47, 57–58, 64, 68, 80
Horns of Consecration, The, viii, xiii, 4, 20–22, 33–34, 38–40, 47–49, 68–69. *See also* Taurus, The Horns of

Illiad, 58
Isis, 54, 69
Isopata, 26

Kairatos, stream of, 19, 28
Kerlescan, 14
Knowth at Newgrange, 9–11, 14, 68
kore, maiden, 37
Kore, goddess, 7, 24
Kouretes, 48, 54

Labyrinth, 18, 25–26, 37, 44–45, 55, 59
Lebor na h Uidre or The Book of the Dun Cow, 15
Lenaia, festival of Dionysus, 53
Leo, constellation, 22, 29
Lesser Mysteries of Eleusinian Mysteries, 54
Lion Gate at Mycenae, 41
"Little Palace" at Knossos, 19
louch, adding water to wine, 54
Lustral Basin, 18, 19, 27–28, 38, 40, 45

Machrie Moor, 14
Maenads, xv, 53, 55–56
Maen yu daus, 13
Maeve, Warrior Queen of Connacht, xv, 51, 60–63, 70
Mars, planet, 56, 80–83, 85
Mars, god of war, 59
Matrona, xiv
Megaron of the Villa at Knossos, 19, 28, 45
Merrivale, 13
Merry Maidens, 13
Messara Valley, 36
Metempsychosis, xv, 63–65
Meton, 66, 67
Metonic Cycle, 66–67, 78
Miletus, 67
Milky Way, 39
"Miniature Fresco of the Sacred Grove and Dance" at Knossos, 19, 26, 42
Minos, 26, 28, 42–45, 47, 88, 91
Minotaur, 44
Mokhlos, 36
"Mother of the Mountains", 28
Mt. Dicte, 40
Mt. Ida, 40

Mt. Juktas, 20, 40, 88, 92
Mycenae, 17, 18, 21, 28, 33, 34–36, 40–42, 49
Mycenaean Linear B Tablets, xiv, 42, 46–48

Naxos, Island of, 25, 45, 55
Nemean Lion, 29–30
North East Hall at Knossos, 23
Northern Entrance Passage at Knossos, 41–42
Nutation, the wobble of the moon, xii, 10–14, 20, 67, 70

Odysseus 58, 63
Odyssey, 58, 63
Oedipus, 30
Oikos or center, 23
Ophiuchus, constellation, 22–23
Orchomenus, 56
Orthus, son of Echidne, 30
Osiris, 54
Ovid, 25
Ozieri, 5

Parapegma, 66–67, 69
Pasiphaë, 26, 43–45
Penelope, Odysseus' wife, 58
Persephone, 7, 24, 54
Pillar Crypt at Knossos, 20, 38, 40–41, 45, 52
Pisces, constellation, 2, 80, 81
Pleiades, star cluster, 39–40, 46, 55, 67, 81
Podei, 4
Porphyry, 6–7
Poseidon, 18, 44, 73
po-ti-ni-ja, title of the goddess, xiv, 24
Priam of Troy, 58
Priestesses' Villa at Knossos, 26, 45
"Prince with the Lillies" fresco at Knossos, 24, 52
Procession Fresco at Knossos, 28, 36
Psychro, cave of, 29
Ptolemy, Claudius, 54, 67
Pylos, 26, 47–48

"Queen's Megaron" at Knossos, 28

Regulus, primary star of Leo, 29
Ring of Brodgar, 14
"Ring of Minos", 21, 38
"Ring of Nestor", 29–30
Royal Draught Board at Knossos, 49, 62–63
Royal Road at Knossos, 19, 40

Sacred Marriage, xiv, 21–22, 24, 44–45, 48, 53, 55, 59
Sacred Pillar, 41, 46
Semele, xv, 53
Sequani Calendar, The, 67–68, 70, 73, 95. *See also* Coligny Calendar
Serpent Bearer and The Serpents, The; Ophiuchus, constellation, 22–23, 25
Serpens Caput, constellation, 22–23
Serpens Cauda, constellation, 22–23
Sethi, tomb of, 69
Shrine of the Double Axes at Knossos, 38, 40
Skiraphorion, lunar Greek calendar month of, 52, 73
Sophocles, 6–7
Sounion, Temple of, 18
sparagmos, ripping and eating of raw flesh, 56
Sphinx, xiv-xv, 27–31, 37
Stones of Stenness, 13–14
Stonehenge, xiii, 2, 6, 9, 11–14, 19, 39–40, 66, 69, 87, 89, 92
Summer Solstice, 22–23, 25, 52, 58–59, 86

Táin Bó Cuailnge, viii, xv, 51, 60–61, 89, 92
Taliesin, Welsh Bard, xv, 15, 51, 64–65, 89, 92
tarb feis, Celtic bull sacrifice, 58–59
Taurean Age, 2, 33

Taurus Mountains, 3
Taurus, The Horns of, vii, xvi, 9, 18, 22, 37, 39, 46, 56–57, 67, 69, 71, 86
Telemachus, Odysseus' son, 58
temenea, sacred spaces, 18
temenos, a sacred space, 19–20, 24, 40
Temple Repositories at Knossos, 23, 45
Temple Wood, 13–14
Thebes, 30, 56
Theseus, 24–25, 27, 45, 55
Thrace, 56
Throne Room at Knossos, 22, 26, 28–29, 37–38, 40, 45, 49
Tiryns, 21
Titans, 29
Tossen-Keler, 14
Tregeseal East, 13
Tripartite Shrine at Knossos, 45
Trojan War, 51, 58
Tuan, 15
Typhon, Titan, 29

Vapheio Tomb, 42–43
Venus, 2, 86
Venus of Laussel, 1
Vergil, 54
Vernal Equinox, 2, 56, 58
Virgo, constellation, 57

Winter Solstice, xvi, 11, 22, 29, 35, 37, 39–40, 46, 67–68, 71, 78, 86
World Tree, 29–30, 41–42, 46, 56, 59–60, 68. *See also* Sacred Pillar

xoana, goddess statue, 23, 40, 45

*yera, Goddess of the Year, 35

Zakros, Palace at, 28, 47
zeugos, the sacrifice of two bulls, 47
Zeus, viii, 24, 27–28, 35, 43, 47–48, 51–54, 57

About the Authors

Helen Benigni (1954–   ) graduated with a Ph.D. in American Literature from Indiana University of Pennsylvania in 1989. She is a Full Professor at Davis and Elkins College in Elkins, West Virginia where she teaches composition, literature, and comparative mythology. The first book she wrote is entitled *The Myth of the Year: Returning to the Origin of the Druid Calendar* (Lanham: University Press of America, 2003); it reveals the astronomy underlying Celtic and Greek mythology using the calendar of the Sequani Druids discovered in Coligny, France and the Sacred Calendar of Eleusis of ancient Greece. She is also the writer of *The Goddess and the Bull: A Study in Minoan-Mycenaean Mythology.*

Barbara Carter (1941–   ) graduated with a B.A. in sociology from the University of Colorado in 1967 where she also did extensive graduate work. She is a professional astrologer and owner of Grouse Haven Astrology located in Elkins, West Virginia. Each year she publishes The Sequani Calendar and manages the website for The Sequani Calendar Group which is at: www.sequanicalendar.com. She is the inventiveness behind the astronomy, the calculations and contributing ideas for both *The Myth of the Year* and *The Goddess and the Bull.*